BLACK&DECKER®

The Complete Guide to a
BETTER LAWN

How to Plant, Maintain & Improve Your Yard & Lawn

by Chris Peterson

Creative Publishing
international

MINNEAPOLIS, MINNESOTA
www.creativepub.com

Creative Publishing
international

Copyright © 2011
Creative Publishing international, Inc.
400 First Avenue North, Suite 300
Minneapolis, Minnesota 55401
1-800-328-0590
www.creativepub.com

Printed in U.S.A.

10 9 8 7 6 5 4 3 2 1

Library of Congress Cataloging-in-Publication Data

The complete guide to a better lawn : how to plant, maintain &
improve your yard & lawn / created by the editors of Creative
Publishing international, Inc., in cooperation with Black & Decker.
      p. cm.
  At head of title: Branded by Black & Decker.
  Summary: "An up-to-date, environmentally responsible approach
to lawn care with mainstream appeal. An ideal reference for busy
homeowners who want better grass quickly and easily"--Provided
by publisher.
  Includes index.
  ISBN-13: 978-1-58923-600-4 (soft cover)
  ISBN-10: 1-58923-600-9 (soft cover)
  1. Lawns. I. Creative Publishing International. II. Black & Decker
Corporation (Towson, Md.) III. Title: How to plant, maintain &
improve your yard & lawn.
  SB433.C66 2011
  635.9'647--dc22
                                    2010050832

President/CEO: Ken Fund

Home Improvement Group

Publisher: Bryan Trandem
Senior Editor: Mark Johanson
Managing Editor: Tracy Stanley

Creative Director: Michele Lanci-Altomare
Senior Design Manager: Jon Simpson, Brad Springer, James Kegley

Lead Photographer: Joel Schnell
Shop Manager: James Parmeter

Production Manager: Laura Hokkanen, Linda Halls

Author: Chris Peterson
Page Layout Artist: Danielle Smith
Technical Editor: David Griffin
Shop Help: Charles Boldt
Prooreader: Drew Siqveland
Editorial Intern: John Buckeye

The Complete Guide to a Better Lawn
Created by: The Editors of Creative Publishing international, Inc., in cooperation with Black & Decker.
Black & Decker® is a trademark of The Black & Decker Corporation and is used under license.

NOTICE TO READERS

For safety, use caution, care, and good judgment when following the procedures described in this book. The publisher and Black & Decker cannot assume responsibility for any damage to property or injury to persons as a result of misuse of the information provided.

The techniques shown in this book are general techniques for various applications. In some instances, additional techniques not shown in this book may be required. Always follow manufacturers' instructions included with products, since deviating from the directions may void warranties. The projects in this book vary widely as to skill levels required: some may not be appropriate for all do-it-yourselfers, and some may require professional help.

Consult your local building department for information on building permits, codes, and other laws as they apply to your project.

Contents

The Complete Guide to a
Better Lawn

Contents (Cont.)

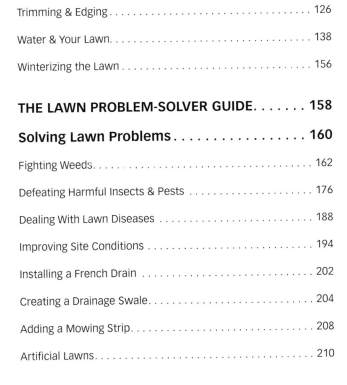

Introduction

Few things make a home look as spectacular as a lush, manicured, emerald green lawn. Aside from making your neighbors green with envy, a fabulous lawn is also the grand, comfortable stage for many of life's most treasured moments, from summer birthday parties, to a lazy neighborhood cookout, to junior's first game of catch with dad. But just as a gorgeous lawn enhances your home, one that has some obvious shortcomings will detract from the look of a house—and the neighborhood in general. A weed-strewn, scraggly, patchy lawn or a sickly plot of grass can bring down the value of the home it's connected to, and it makes outdoor activities less enjoyable.

There's simply no reason to put up with a less-than-wonderful lawn. Dense, healthy turf doesn't materialize by accident. It's the result of timely feeding, watering, and regular maintenance. Conscientious lawn care not only creates a luxurious carpet of grass, it is also your first and easiest line of defense against weeds, insects, disease and other lawn problems. Preventing them from occurring is always easier than dealing with them after they rear their ugly heads.

That's why we've laid out all the basics of lawn maintenance in this book, including exactly what you need to do to keep your lawn healthy, and when you need to do it.

Of course even the most meticulously tended lawns occasionally have an outbreak of weeds, a problem with grubs, or even a small patch of dollar spot fungus. After all, you can't entirely control nature. So we've also included a comprehensive "Lawn Problem-Solving Guide" in this book, ensuring that you always have the right solution for whatever problem crops up.

Keeping ahead of lawn problems and on top of your lawn's needs entails just a little diligence and the right knowledge and advice. It's not hard. You provide the watchful eye and few hours on weekends, and these pages will serve up the information you need to create a verdant, rich green lawn that you and your family can enjoy with pride.

Gallery of Beautiful Lawns

Y ou can learn a lot about lawns just by looking at them. The color is the first thing that sticks out. A healthy, well-fed, and well-tended lawn will be a deep consistent green. And it's not just the color; a healthy lawn is also dense and cut suitably high so that it has the welcoming appeal and magnetism of a plush carpet. You just want to lie down on it.

Take a stroll down your block and you may find that precious few yards actually look this inviting. That's because many different elements come together in the creation of a truly memorable lawn. In addition to a sharp appearance of its own, the lawn should also complement the edges of the property and visually complement other yard features, such as flowerbeds, shrubs and trees.

That said, growing the better lawn is not a great mystery, it's the product of a little thought, a little time, and making sure the lawn is kept healthy. If it's kept in fighting trim, you lawn will do the rest—filling out in a dense mat of eye-catching green and looking good even in periods of drought, overuse, or less-than-ideal weather.

The following pages feature inspiring lawns that show what a little work and quick action in dealing with the occasional pest, weed, and disease can do. These examples should provide ample motivation for you to create your own little carpet of heaven right outside your front—or back—door.

Healthy Turf

An in-ground sprinkler system, although somewhat expensive and labor-intensive to install, can save a significant amount of time, money, and hassle over the years.

Mowing patterns are a wonderful and easy way to add a fascinating graphic element to your healthy lawn.

A lush, pristine lawn like this requires excellent soil, ideal conditions, and dedicated lawn maintenance.

A blanket of healthy turf grass not only looks beautiful, but is a highly effective way to prevent soil erosion in a hilly lawn area.

There's nothing wrong with this lawn; allowing a cool-season lawn to go dormant helps keep it healthy and, as long it's mowed trim as this lawn has been, it can still look nice and tidy.

This southern lawn has been mowed extremely low to achieve an elegant, velvety texture. Only a few grass species will tolerate mowing to such a short height; mow the correct height for your lawn.

Healthy grass grows vigorously as long as it gets plenty of sun and water. Keeping up with the growth takes some effort but will give payback in many ways because healthier plants are much more resistant to disease and they outperform weeds.

A well-maintained lawn can be identified in a quick glance in most cases. The urge to take off your shoes and run through the grass is a key sign that you're doing a good job in the lawn care department.

Beautiful Borders

Crisp edging goes a long way toward helping a lawn look spiffy. Keeping edges cut cleanly will also help prevent healthy lawn grasses from invading flowerbeds.

A gravel pathway separates the lawn from adjacent shrub beds. A matching brick border separates the gravel path from the lawn, ensuring that the edge can be easily mown without the fear of flying gravel.

Lawn-edge pathways not only add a distinctive design element to any lawn, they are also extremely practical. They limit the need for edging, make mowing easier, and keep aggressive garden plants from invading the grass—and vice versa.

Accent Plantings

From container plants to meticulously pruned shrubs to wildflowers, border plantings, specimen trees, and climbing vines, this yard features just about every imaginable type of accent plant. The element that ties it all together: a lush green lawn.

Ornamental rose gardens are lovely counterpoints to this strip of lawn, but the homeowner has to keep a watchful eye on the lawn's soil. The Japanese beetles that are common rose pests can start as white grub infestations in the lawn. Protecting lawn health often means being aware of what other plants are nearby.

Climbing roses add life and color to the transition area between this stretch of lawn and the driveway. The plants also help soften the hard lines of the metal railing for a more inviting appearance.

A beautiful flowering cherry tree, low-lying shrubs, and flowering ground covers thrive in a high-traffic corner where the grass struggled to survive. The solution to a lawn problem often lies in being creative with landscape plantings.

Because this lawn has essentially been designed as the pathway between flower beds, the grass chosen is one that is tolerant to high traffic. Always consider if your grass species is well suited to the plans you have for your yard and landscape.

Native wildflowers planted around the edges of this lawn create an informal border that feels natural and requires only minimal maintenance.

The right tree can be a lovely addition and a great way to break up an otherwise boring expanse of lawn. But choose carefully. The tree should have a modest canopy and it should be placed where the sun will move around it during the day, preventing lawn thinning due to lack of sun.

Hardscape Helpers

Mowing strips, such as the concrete versions shown here, save you time and effort spent edging. They also add a sharp look to the lawn.

A wonderful stepping-stone path leads visitors through the yard and prevents soil compaction and grass damage from foot traffic. Stepping-stone paths are the easiest to install in a lawn, and can save a lot of wear and tear.

It's often wiser to terrace a severe slope than to try to grow grass there. This low-maintenance terrace garden replaced a section of lawn that was both difficult to keep healthy and a challenge to mow.

An elegant stepping-stone pathway leads both the eye and foot traffic to a lovely outdoor patio. It also prevents that foot traffic from causing lawn compaction.

A mixed bag of masonry structures could easily be a visual mess, but the calm tones of this plush lawn provide a resting place for the eye and allow each stone or brick element to stand on its own. For the record, this landscape includes poured concrete steps, a curved concrete paver walkway, a mortared fieldstone wall, a mortarless ashlar wall with flagstone cap, and a brick wall.

A rock garden and a garden pond with stone coping provide shape and form to this landscape. The gardens create rounded forms and interesting irregular lines in the lawn borders that give it a very organic feeling.

Evaluating Your Lawn

Before you can really meet your lawn's needs, you have to know what those needs are. The grass in your lawn may be any of a dozen different common types, each with its own nutritional and maintenance requirements. The soil beneath your lawn can be rich loam, quick-draining sand, or impenetrable clay—or any combination. Certain weeds, pests, and diseases will be common to your area. Growing the best lawn possible entails knowing all you can about the grass, local conditions, and the problems your lawn is likely to face and why.

Understanding your lawn starts with the soil. Determining which nutrients are present, and which are missing, will help you choose precisely the type and quantity of fertilizer your lawn needs to grow as robustly as possible.

The type of grass is as important as the soil. With that in mind, we've provided a visual guide to lawn grasses. This will allow you to come up with a maintenance plan tailored to your yard, and develop strategies for heading off problems such as pests and disease long before they take hold.

A simple and comprehensive lawn-care plan is the ultimate goal of any thorough lawn assessment, which is exactly what you should have once you're finished with this chapter.

In this chapter:
- Understanding Your Soil
- Lawn Soil Types
- Soil Nutrients
- Testing Your Soil
- Knowing Your Lawn
- Geography, Climate & Grass Choice
- Cool-Season Grasses
- Warm-Season Grasses
- Inspecting Your Lawn
- Your Lawn-Care Plan
- Scheduling Lawn Care

Understanding Your Soil

A lush, healthy lawn begins with the soil that lies beneath it. Good soil is your first line of defense against problems, because it ensures that the grass has all the nutrients it needs to grow strong, win the competition against weeds, deny pests a home, and prevent disease. The best soil also ensures that water drains quickly enough so that the lawn doesn't drown, but not so quickly that it dies of thirst.

How well your soil supports lawn growth and health depends on the balance of the four basic ingredients that make up any soil: air, water, inorganic minerals, and organic matter—the mix of decaying plants and insects called humus. The wrong balance creates a soil that doesn't drain and discourages root growth, or one that drains too quickly to effectively hold nutrients. The right balance is a rich mixture teeming with beneficial life.

Lawns prefer loam for good reason. Loam provides a ready supply of nutrients to the grass. Those nutrients, like the soil structure itself, must be in proper balance to ensure that the lawn gets the food it needs, when it needs it. The three main nutrients you'll encounter most often in discussions of lawn health are nitrogen, phosphorous, and potassium. But as essential as these are, they are only a few of the many nutrients present in healthy soil. An overabundance or deficiency of other key nutrients can create problems just as serious as an imbalance in the big three.

The nutrients available to grass roots will also be affected by the pH of the soil, which is the measure of how acidic it is. An imbalance in pH can occur when a lawn is not correctly maintained, or is improperly fertilized. When soil becomes too acidic or alkaline (the opposite of acidity), some nutrients become unavailable. It's easy to fix an acidity imbalance, but detecting it early is key. Maintaining proper pH, along with ensuring the right balance of nutrients, is why any sensible lawn program starts with a basic soil test.

How well the soil supports your lawn also depends on how much soil you actually have. Topsoil that is more than five inches deep provides an excellent foundation for the typical lawn. But topsoil is expensive, which is why home builders and contractors often use two inches or less. That can translate to a lawn that struggles. So in addition to making sure your soil is supplying the proper nutrients to the grass, you'll also need to determine how much soil you've got to work with. In most cases, it's a good idea to regularly add organic matter on top of the lawn to build up the soil base, in a process called topdressing.

But whatever you do, always keep in mind that although you can't see it, the soil underneath your lawn is just as important as the grass itself. It's a living, breathing thing, and keeping the soil healthy is key to keeping your lawn healthy.

Rich loam is the soil of choice for lawns; different size particles, a wealth of decomposing organic materials, and beneficial organisms ensure grass roots get the nutrients, water, and air they need.

Lawn Soil Types

When we talk of soil, we are really discussing the relatively thin layer of topsoil that sits atop a much deeper layer of subsoil. The topsoil is the layer in which plants can grow; subsoil is unfit for plant growth. But the subsoil can affect the chemistry of the topsoil, most specifically, the pH. The other important factor in the makeup of topsoil is location.

Soil differs greatly from one geographic region to another, but all soil falls into one of three classifications: clay, loam, or sand. If you live in certain parts of the south, you may have to deal with distinctively clay-heavy soil, while homes in coastal areas often struggle with extremely sandy soils. Loam is the most desirable soil. Clay drains poorly and the dense structure resists root growth. Sandy soil drains much too quickly to hold the nutrients necessary to keep the lawn healthy.

No matter what type of soil is natural to your area, soil health and structure also depend on how the lawn has been used over time, and how it has been maintained. For instance, a lawn that has seen many years of hard use as a football field for a growing group of kids will likely be tightly compacted and dense. An excess of certain nutrients such as calcium can also adversely impact soil structure, as can an imbalance of other nutrients.

However, most lawn soils are not totally one type or the other. If you look closely at your soil, it's likely you'll see a mix, such as a sandy loam. That's why the goal of improvements like aerating the lawn, and adding structural amendments such as compost, is to create a soil that is most conducive to a healthy lawn.

Determining Your Soil Texture ▶

Soils partly come from the earth's mineral crust and partly from the remains of living things. The mineral (inorganic) part is rock that has been worn down to particles. **Clay** (left photo) is simply stone that has worn down to microscopically small particles. Clay soils are dense and slow draining. Clay soils compact easily when wet. Compacted clay soils resist root penetration and do not support grass well. Most clay soils form a tight wad when squeezed in your hand that does not easily crumble.

The inorganic part of **Loam** soils (center photo) are a mixture of clay, silt, and sand particles. Loam is the best soil for lawns since it doesn't compact like clay or dry out like sand. A handful of moist loam will form a ball when squeezed, but the ball will crumble as you handle it.

Sand soils (right photo) are gritty and resist forming a cohesive ball. Sand soil resists compaction better than clay and loam but dries out quickly unless generously amended with organic matter. Heavy clay and dry sand soils are best improved with the addition of compost or other organic matter.

Soil Nutrients

Soil serves as the lawn's kitchen. A rich, healthy soil provides a smorgasbord of varying amounts of more than a dozen macro and micronutrients. These range from large amounts of nitrogen to trace amounts of copper and zinc. However, the main courses and the nutrients you're most likely to deal with and adjust are nitrogen, phosphorous, and potassium (denoted by the initials N-P-K).

Nitrogen is considered the biggest player in that trio, because its effects are most apparent. Largely responsible for lawn growth and the deep green color that marks a vigorous lawn, nitrogen spurs the process of photosynthesis by which the grass plant actually feeds itself. Available nitrogen is used up or washes out of the soil very quickly, but too much nitrogen applied all at once can cause more problems than it addresses, including "burning" the lawn, killing off beneficial organisms in the soil, and creating very rapid blade growth at the expense of proper root development. Fortunately, there are many available sources for nitrogen, from fine lawn clippings themselves to natural fertilizers, to the synthetic mixes sold at most garden centers. The trick is to feed the lawn a steady and moderate supply of nitrogen.

Phosphorous is important in its own right, primarily for aiding root and shoot growth. Most soils typically contain enough phosphorous to feed a lawn, but in unhealthy soils, the nutrient can be bound up and unavailable to the root system.

Potassium is the unsung hero in your soil. It acts as a vitamin and supplement to your lawn, helping the grass plants block out weed growth, resist disease, and tolerate stressors such as cold snaps and drought. Unfortunately, a lack of potassium is a hard thing to discern, which is why it's usually a part of any regular lawn feeding.

As important as these big three are, keep in mind that the key to healthy soil is balance. If only a single nutrient is out of whack, it can negatively affect how other nutrients are absorbed by lawn.

The Perfect pH ▸

Soil acidity is measured on a 14-point pH scale. On this scale, 1 is extremely acidic, 7 is neutral and 14 is extremely alkaline. Lawn soil should generally be neutral or slightly acidic, falling somewhere between 6.5 and 7 on the scale. Soil that is too acidic or too alkaline (the opposite of acidity) will hinder lawn health. Depending on how severe the imbalance is, acidity or alkalinity will "lock up" certain nutrients making them unavailable to the lawn.

Lawn soil acidity can be affected by local geographic conditions, the age of the lawn, the type of fertilizers that have been used, and other factors. Soil that that is too acidic can be remedied with the application of lime, while alkaline soils can be corrected by adding sulfur to the soil. But these corrections have to be done very carefully.

In any case, the place to start is with a soil test, as described on page 30. In addition to measuring the relative levels of different nutrients in the soil, the test should accurately depict the pH level. Keep in mind when reading your results that the scale is exponential: a one-point difference in the scale—say, from 6 to 5—represents a tenfold increase in acidity or alkalinity.

Not Just For Bait Anymore ▸

Keep an eye out for earthworms in your lawn soil. These wriggly little creatures are a sure sign of healthy soil, because they process decaying matter and create waste, or "castings," that add to the nutrients your lawn uses to make its own food. They will not proliferate in an unhealthy soil base, and a lack of earthworms is oftentimes the "canary in the coal mine" of your lawn's health.

Thinking Green: Composting ▸

Gardeners call compost "black gold," because not only does it provide a nutrient-rich, structure-improving soil amendment that few fertilizers can rival, composting is also a low- or no-cost way to recycle household and yard waste, keeping it out of landfills while benefiting your lawn.

Among the many wonderful attributes of compost is that it releases its nutrients slowly for long-term benefits. And even if you add other fertilizers to your lawn, compost-enriched soil will bind those fertilizers, limiting runoff and stopping excess fertilizer from making its way into sewage streams, waterways, and watersheds.

You can buy compost from most garden centers, but it's almost as easy to make your own. Purchase one of the many prefabricated compost bins on the market, or build your own with straw bales, wood, chicken wire, or any material that will create an enclosure that allows for air circulation. You can even just pile layers of different yard and kitchen waste in a discrete corner of the yard. For quick results, turn the pile every couple of weeks to make sure it's kept moist. Even a neglected pile will eventually become your own little source of black gold!

Testing Your Soil

Rush out to buy fertilizer, amendments, or lawn-care products of any sort without knowing what's already in your soil, and you're flying blind. That's where soil tests come in.

A decent soil test kit (look to pay $20 or more) will tell you if your pH is off. It will also measure relative amounts of nitrogen, phosphorous, and potassium in the soil. That information will give you a great start on determining whether or not you need to immediately make corrections. A soil test provides a great overview snapshot of your soil health, and you can use the test results to select the appropriate fertilizer blend for your lawn (that's if you determine you even need to fertilize at all). You'll find home test kits that give you results right away at large home centers and nurseries.

Mail-in kits provide more accurate and more comprehensive information, including levels of soluble salts in the soil and percentages of micronutrients. Some even provide recommendations for correcting soil imbalances. You'll wait a few weeks for the results and you'll have to spend a little bit more money for mail-in tests. But if you have doubts about the health of your soil or have detected multiple problems in the lawn, a mail-in test kit is probably the way to go. You can find mail-in kits online, or get them through your local cooperative extension office. The Cooperative Extension System (now called the National Institute for Food and Agriculture) is a federal government agency with a network of regional branch offices throughout every state in the nation. Charged with advancing knowledge about agriculture, the environment, and related issues, your local extension office offers soil testing as part of their services. Collect a soil sample as shown in the steps on page 31, but put the sample in the container supplied by the extension office. Mail the sample to the lab in the mailer provided, and you'll receive a highly detailed report.

Look to test your soil in the early spring, after the weather first turns warm, or in the late fall, after the lawn has gone dormant. Make sure to create your sample from several different areas of the lawn, and carefully follow the directions that come with the test kit.

Jar Test ▶

You can tell what texture soil you're working with by conducting a jar test. Fill a quart jar two-thirds full with water. Gradually add to the jar a soil sample from the desired planting area. Continue adding soil until water reaches the top of the jar. Cover and shake, then allow the sediment to settle for a day. The sand will settle first, then silt, and finally clay. Is your soil predominantly sand? Mostly clay?

Heavy clay soils and dry sand soils are most effectively improved by the addition of organic matter. While it would seem that adding sand should make a clay soil more like loam, in practice this mixture produces hard, brick-like chunks in the soil. Instead, till in generous quantities of peat, compost, or composted manure. Contact your local extension service for recommendations on the best kinds and quantities of organic matter to add to your clay or sand soils.

How to Test Your Soil

Clean a thin garden trowel and gallon bucket with a mild soap mixture. Wipe them with a clean, dry cloth moistened with rubbing alcohol. Allow them to dry before gathering the soil.

Dig up samples from different areas of the lawn. Half a trowel of dirt or less from each of about five or six locations will be plenty.

Collect the soil in the bucket as you go. When you've collected the soil you'll need, use the trowel to thoroughly blend the soil samples.

Test the soil for key nutrients and acidity, using the test kit tubes, and following the kit's instructions.

Knowing Your Lawn

A lawn is a garden unto itself, typically populated by over a million grass plants that are all incredibly alike in their structure and growing habits. Those plants are fairly special; of the thousands upon thousands of grass species, only a select group of about 50 are suitable for use in a lawn.

All turfgrass species share a basic structure. Turfgrasses grow from a central node at ground level called a crown. The crown is essentially the main control center of the plant. It sucks up water and nutrients from the roots to fuel the process of photosynthesis in the leaves by which any turfgrass produces its own food. That food is then used to generate both root and leaf growth. Amazingly, even if you severely scalp the top growth and the roots are underfed, dried out, and shriveled up, your grass still has a fighting chance if the crown is intact.

Sturdy stems called shoots grow out of the crown with a protective covering known as a sheath. Each stem is capable of producing several growth nodes, out of which new leaves will sprout. Most people call these leaves blades (technically speaking, only the top portion of the leaf), and the fact that you can cut them again and again without damaging the plant is something that makes grass unique among plants. It's also the trait that allows you to mow regularly.

Turfgrasses differ in how they grow and spread. Like other grasses, turfgrasses will reproduce by going to seed if you allow them to. But routine lawn mowing prevents this from happening. Instead, turfgrasses grow new plants in one of three ways. Rhizomatous grasses create new growth at the end of underground stems, called rhizomes. Stoloniferous grasses produce new plants at nodes along stolons, essentially rhizomes that creep along aboveground setting new plants down into the soil. Clumping grasses don't send out stolons; they grow new stems called tillers, directly out of the crown. The bushy growth habit is why clump grasses are sometimes called bush or bunch grasses.

The reason this distinction matters to homeowners is because stoloniferous and rhizomatous grasses tend to fill out more quickly and fully, making for a lusher lawn. That's why they are the most popular varieties for lawns.

Turfgrasses can be classified as annual or perennial, but the vast majority of lawns are perennial grasses. It's not very useful to have your lawn die out every year. The more important division is seasonality. Some grasses grow best in warmer parts (called warm-season grasses) of the country, while others thrive in cooler areas (called, predictably, cool-season grasses).

Knowing what grass species you have, how it spreads, and what season it prefers determines when you should fertilize and water, how you should mow and maintain the lawn, and what pests and problems you can expect to battle.

Some turfgrass plants grow out from a central crown that provides moisture and nutrients to the leaves so that essential photosynthesis can occur.

Turf Grass Propagation

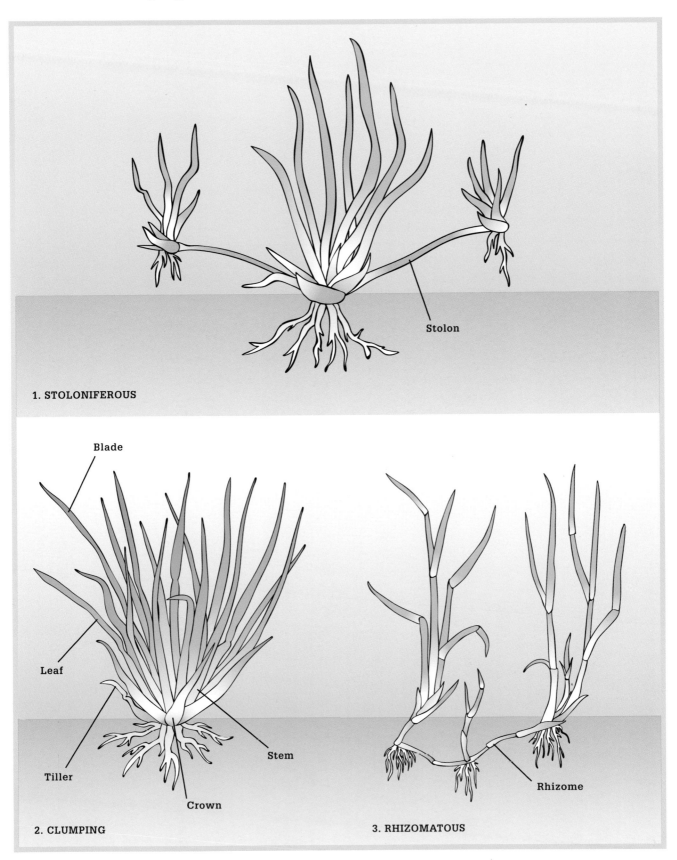

1. STOLONIFEROUS

Stolon

Blade

Leaf

Tiller

Crown

Stem

2. CLUMPING

Rhizome

3. RHIZOMATOUS

Geography, Climate & Grass Choice

Just as you select the flowers, vegetables, trees and shrubs for your yard and garden based largely on your climate, you need to choose turfgrass that thrives in your yard. Like any other plant, turfgrass has its own needs and characteristics, including relative tolerance to sun and shade, heat preferences, and water requirements. The type of seed or sod you select for lawn planting or renovation should not be chosen based simply on whether you live in a cool or warm part of the country, but should take into account regional variations. Fortunately, there is a very good resource to help you do just that.

The map below is a representation of the Turfgrass Climate Zone Map developed by the United States National Arboretum. Similar to the American Horticultural Society Heat Zone Map that gardeners often use, this map divides the country into five separate zones. The characteristics of each zone determine which turfgrass or grasses will do best in that zone. You may find other turfgrass zone maps; seed companies sometimes develop their own to reflect the species and varieties they have developed. But this version is the most common and, for most purposes, it's a very effective resource in choosing the specific grass that will work best in your location.

The map breaks the country into the following five zones:

Cool arid (1). Encompassing such a large geographic region, it should be no surprise that this zone features an incredible diversity of microclimates. Mild, snowy-to-dry winters are the flip side of warm-to-very hot, dry summers. The diversity of this zone makes it a good idea to contact your local cooperative extension office or university agricultural program for help in choosing just the right grass. Kentucky bluegrass is one of the most common to this region and will do well, but given the relatively modest rainfall throughout the zone, you should plan on regular watering for best growth.

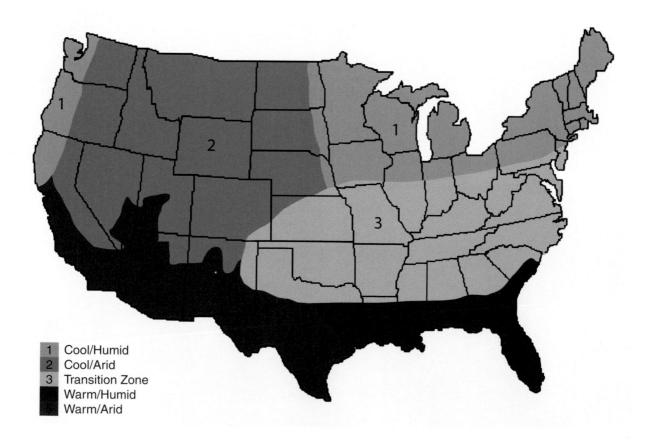

1 Cool/Humid
2 Cool/Arid
3 Transition Zone
  Warm/Humid
  Warm/Arid

Cool humid (2). Another diverse zone, this is a region of extremes. Within the boundaries of this zone, there are frigid-to-mild winters, and hot to temperate summers. But moisture comes with all seasons. Most of the cool-season grasses do well in this zone.

Warm humid (3). A typical southern region, this zone features uniformly mild, wet winters, and hot, humid summers. The abundance of moisture provides a breeding ground for insects and a hospitable environment for many different lawn diseases, so vigilance is key in this zone. Treat any problems with the appropriate solution as soon as signs of disease become apparent. Bermuda grass, St. Augustine grass, and zoysia grass all do well in this region.

Warm arid (4). This is perhaps the most difficult region in which to maintain a lush, dense, and deep green lawn. The big challenge is, of course, water; options such as in-ground sprinklers, drip hoses and grey water systems are all part of lawn care here. The most common species throughout this zone is Bermuda grass.

Transition zone (5). Running along the center of the country from the east coast to around Missouri, this zone represents the most challenging area for growing turfgrass. Harsh summers and freezing winters mean that neither cool-season nor warm-season grasses are going to do well everywhere in the zone. The answer is to use Interstate 80 as a dividing line. If you're north of that line, cool-season grasses such as perennial ryegrass will probably work best in your yard. If you're south of the line, and experience milder winters, consider growing Bermuda grass.

Understanding Microclimates ▸

The Turfgrass Climate Zone Map is an excellent tool, but it can't account for all geographic elevations and variations. Certain "microclimates" sometimes feature completely different conditions than the zone within which they are located. If your home is located within a microclimate, you need to take that into account when choosing seed or sod.

A microclimate is created when a local feature causes a small area to experience much different conditions than the surrounding geography. For instance, if you live in the cool/arid zone, but your home is located in a deep valley where fog is common in the summer, it's likely that you could consider a less drought-tolerant species than could survive elsewhere in your region. Likewise, if your yard is shaded most of the day and is at the foot of a watershed slope, you'll have much wetter conditions than your neighbors.

Being aware of your local and site conditions helps you further refine your choice of turfgrass, and can play a large part in just how well your particular grass grows.

Local conditions such as frequent snowfall and freezing temperatures will affect what grass type you should overseed with or plant in the first place.

Cool-Season Grasses

One of the best ways to head off potential problems with your lawn, and avoid extra work in keeping it as healthy as possible, is to select the right grass from the start. The first step in making that decision is choosing between cool-season and warm-season grasses.

Simply put, cool-season grasses grow best in colder climates, while warm-season species do better in warm areas. Cool-season grasses prefer temperatures between 60 and 75°F and require a significant and steady supply of water to grow their best. Kentucky bluegrass is the most common cool-season grass, chosen for its attractive blades, strong growth, and resistance to disease. However, cool-season lawns are typically comprised of a mix of species.

The schedule of maintenance is where the differences between cool- and warm-season turfgrasses really become most apparent. Cool-season lawns grow most vigorously in the cool of spring and the chill of early fall. As the heat of summer comes on, or during unusual hot spells in other seasons when the temperature is consistently above 85° F, cool-season lawns will actually go dormant. This may include turning brown if the climate is dry and hot without respite for more than a week or so.

Consequently, you'll need to mow a cool-season lawn much more frequently in the spring and fall, and may not need to mow at all for several weeks in the middle of a hot summer. Periods of growth and dormancy also affect when you should fertilize the lawn (see page 94), and the best time for undertaking stressful procedures such as dethatching.

Although you won't have to do frequent mowing on a cool-season lawn during hot summer months, you will have to increase your vigilance. The stress of heat and the diminished activity of dormancy leave cool-season grasses susceptible to damage from drought-related diseases such as dollar spot. It also leaves the lawn vulnerable to infestation from pests, and poorly equipped to withstand simple damage such as compaction from summer parties and sports.

Winter Help ▶

One of the big disadvantages to many warm-season grasses is that they go brown over the winter. So even though you may live in a southern climate where other plants flourish over the winter months, your lovely green lawn will look dead. A remedy used by many homeowners in warmer states is to overseed the lawn in fall with annual varieties of cool-season species such as ryegrass or fescue. The cool-season grass greens the lawn during the cooler days between fall and spring, and then dies away just as the native warm-season grass greens up with the rising temperatures. This technique also adds to the health of a southern lawn, because the actively growing cool-season grass will crowd out opportunistic weeds.

The best time to overseed a warm-season lawn is when it goes dormant and the temperature is consistently below 75° F. The cool-season grass seed is spread with a spreader after the lawn has been thoroughly raked to remove any loose thatch or debris. Spread the seed in one direction, and then repeat the process in the perpendicular direction. Finally, rake the lawn again to force the seeds down to the soil, and water thoroughly. Water daily until the seedlings take root.

You'll probably need to fertilize over the winter months to keep the lawn at its greenest. When the weather warms and it comes time to let your warm-season grass reassert itself, stop fertilizing, let the lawn go dry, and mow shorter than normal.

Kentucky bluegrass is the most common type of cool-season grass. It is a favorite of northern homeowners because it's beautiful and relatively easy to keep healthy and looking great.

Guide to Popular Cool-Season Grasses ▸

NAME	DESCRIPTION	DROUGHT TOLERANT	MAINTENANCE	MOW HEIGHT	DURABILITY	SPREAD	PROS AND CONS
Kentucky Bluegrass	A rich blue-green color and elegant blade shape are two of the many qualities that make Kentucky bluegrass the most popular cool-season lawn species	No	Med-high	2½"	High	Rhizome	Mixes well with other species; requires a lot of water; slow to establish; not particularly disease- or insect-resistant
Tall Fescue	Dense, coarse appearance, with deep roots, and strong sod structure makes this a favorite for play areas	Yes	Low	3"	High	Clump	Great in high traffic areas; resistant to shade, heat, disease and pests; will thin out in some northern areas
Fine Fescues	Very fine bristle leaves, and a pretty, medium-green color, make the fine fescues (chewings, red, among others) a favorite in cooler northern localities	Yes	Low	2½"	Low	Rhizome and clumps, depending on variety	The fine fescues grow well in shade and in sandy soils; but they do not stand up well to traffic
Bentgrass	Soft, dense and low growing, bentgrass is a plush and appealing choice, often used for tennis courts and putting greens	No	Very High	1"	Med	Stolon	Tolerates scalping (as low as ¼"); quick to recover from damage; blades bend unattractively if allowed to grow too long; frequent watering and mowing
Perennial Ryegrass	Finely textured, glossy deep-green blades, make ryegrass a lovely lawn choice	Slightly	Low	2"	High	Clump	Establishes quickly; very wear tolerant; can't stand up to deep cold

Guide to Popular Transitional Grasses ▸

NAME	DESCRIPTION	DROUGHT TOLERANT	MAINTENANCE	MOW HEIGHT	DURABILITY	SPREAD	PROS AND CONS
Buffalo Grass	A nice gray-green color along with a fine texture and dense growth habit makes this a handsome grass to grow in difficult climates	Yes	Low	3½"	High	Stolons	Disease resistant; tolerant to heat, harsh sun and poor soils; expensive; susceptible to weed growth
Blue Grama	Gray-green color and fine texture make it similar to Buffalo grass; fuzzy blades set it apart	Yes	Low	2½"	Medium	Rhizomes	Tolerates poor soils; easy to care for; slow to green in spring; turns brown in cold; sparse growth

Warm-Season Grasses

Relocate from Massachusetts to Florida, and along with a year-round tan, you'll find a much different lawn outside your front door—it will even look different. Warm-season grasses vary in appearance from species to species far more than cool-season grasses do. Southern grass species range from mat-forming broad-leafed types, to specimens that more closely resemble their northern cousins. This gives the southern homeowner in search of a new turfgrass a wealth of choices.

Appearances aside, the warm-season grasses share a whole slew of characteristics, the traits that fundamentally separate them from cool-season species. Chief among these are growth periods.

As far as warm-season lawns are concerned, the hotter the better. They grow most actively when the temperature is above 80°F, and will keep growing strong right into triple-digit temperatures. This group of grasses basically has an on–off switch: they start growing when the weather gets hot in early summer, and shut down at the first sign of frost in late fall, after which they go completely dormant until late spring.

Unlike their cool-season counterparts, warm-season lawns are usually comprised of a single species of grass. And because of the way they grow, these species are usually planted as sod or plugs, while new cold-season lawns can easily be seeded. The most common warm-season grasses are Bermuda grass and St. Augustine grass, both of which are disease-resistant, and low growing. This limits the amount of mowing you need to do—a big plus when it's hot outside.

Transition Grasses ▸

As you can see on the map on page 34, some areas of the country can't be neatly classified as cool or warm. They're actually a little bit of both. Homes in these transitional areas generally call for very rugged and adaptable lawns that can potentially survive both steaming hot summers and frigid snowy winters. The best transition grasses are actually native grasses that once grew wild on the plains of the Midwest. These include buffalograss and Blue Grama.

A durable and low-maintenance choice, St. Augustine grass can be found throughout most warmer climates, especially in the deep south in the United States.

Guide to Popular Warm-Season Grasses ▸

NAME	DESCRIPTION	DROUGHT TOLERANT	MAINTENANCE	MOW HEIGHT	DURABILITY	SPREAD	PROS AND CONS
St. Augustine	A fast-growing, coarse-textured, standby, St. Augustine is popular in temperate areas that see no cold weather	Slightly	High	2½"	Medium	Stolon	Shade tolerant; susceptible to many pests and diseases and thatch buildup, coarse texture underfoot
Bermuda	Soft, dense and a fetching green, this selection is a low, spreading, tough species	Slightly	High	1½"	High	Rhizomes and stolons	Great for high-traffic areas; will grow in many different types of soil; won't tolerate shade; invasive — protect nearby beds
Bahiagrass	Bright green, coarse, low-growing species that is exceptionally tough	Yes	Low	2"	High	Rhizomes	Extremely resistant to wear; tolerates shade and poor soils; extensive roots prevent erosion; susceptible to certain diseases
Zoysia	Medium textured, dark green grass, thick, dense growth	Yes	Medium	1½"	High	Rhizomes and stolons	Grows in poor soil; tolerant of moderate shade; resistant to pests and diseases; turns straw brown early in winter and stays brown until early summer; prone to thatch
Centipede Grass	Medium textured, light green turfgrass that is low growing and easy to maintain	Yes	Low	2"	Low	Stolons creeping, thus the name	Tolerates partial shade; slow growing means less mowing; tolerates poor soil; quick to turn brown; slow to recover from damage
Carpet Grass	Medium texture, undistinguished form and a light dull green make this a less than stellar choice	No	Low	2½"	Low	Stolons	Shade tolerant; will grow in boggy conditions; quick to turn brown; will not tolerate traffic

Inspecting Your Lawn

A lawn is more than soil and turfgrass. Once the grass takes root, spreads, and becomes established, the grass and soil form an intricate relationship, creating a living carpet that can be negatively affected by many different problems. Some of these, such as fertilizer burn, show up quickly and blatantly. Others, such as thatch buildup, become worse slowly. To catch any problem before it has the chance to profoundly stunt the growth of your lawn, look a little deeper than the surface. A thorough inspection of your lawn starts with slicing out a chunk of the turf and soil and taking a good, hard look in profile, with an eye to all the potential troublespots.

Look first at the top growth. It will tell you whether you're doing everything you need to do to properly maintain the lawn. Are the blades yellow? That may signify a deficiency of iron or nitrogen. Are they ragged at the top? This is a sure sign that you need to sharpen your mower blades, and a potential entry point for disease.

Also look at the base of your grass plants. Thatch buildup (see page 50) can slowly choke out your grass and needs to be remedied before you have a severely weakened lawn that has no energy to prevent opportunistic weeds from taking over. Are the crowns of the plants healthy and producing stolons, rhizomes or tillers? Stunted growth may point to a number of problems.

Of course, what happens below the surface is just as important. A side view of your soil will tell you if pests are trying a sneak attack, or if the lawn is becoming overly compacted from too much foot traffic. Check soil texture to make sure it is not too dense or too loose. This is also your chance to ensure that your grass plants are growing a deep, interconnected, healthy root system.

Whether you find problems or not, a basic inspection of your lawn's structure tells you volumes about what's going on above and below the surface. That's what makes it one of the easiest ways to check on lawn health and get a jump on any problems that do exist.

How to Evaluate Your Lawn

Use a spade or square-edged shovel to cut a wedge out of the lawn. Take the sample from an inconspicuous area of the lawn. Cut at least 6" deep.

Closely examine the soil chunk for any obvious problems, such as burrowing insects, compaction, or conditions that need amendment, such as heavy clay.

Expose the root structure. Ideally, the roots should run at least 4" to 5" deep, and should form an intertwined network. There should be plenty of new, white root growth.

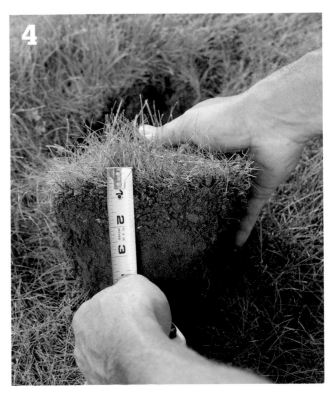

Determine the extent of thatch buildup. Measure to check that the thatch layer is not more than ½" thick or compacted, which indicates the lawn needs to be dethatched.

Inspect individual leaves. Look for signs of disease and discoloration due to malnutrition. Check the tops to ensure the lawn mower blades are cutting cleanly, not tearing.

Replace the wedge from the spot where you dug it out. Tamp it down gently, sprinkle a little soil around the seams, and then water the spot well.

Your Lawn-Care Plan

Whether you're working with an existing lawn or looking to plant a completely new one, a good plan is essential to success. That plan begins with the actual design of the lawn, which should take into account both aesthetic and pragmatic concerns.

Start with the basic contours of your yard, sketching the outline on a pad. Now consider how you want the lawn to fit within the yard. This will be a simple exercise if you are looking for a fairly basic square or rectangle that sets the stage for foundation plantings and the home's architecture. But design-wise, it's always a little more interesting to break up an expanse of lawn with one or more flower beds, trees, a line of shrubs, or other features that create visual variety. Sketch any features you want to add, creating a plant and materials list as necessary, and you'll be all set to modify the design when you're ready to start work.

The design will also be affected by features you add out of necessity or to make the lawn easier to care for. For instance, your planning may include installing mowing strips to circumvent the need for edging, replacing grass on severe slopes with garden terraces to make mowing easier and watering more efficient, or adding stepping stones to protect against soil compaction from foot traffic.

Any lawn-care plan is also likely to include more practical modifications, changes you make just to improve the health of the lawn. Adding new drainage and amending soil before you install a new lawn are both examples of pragmatic improvements that might be part of your master plan.

You'll also want to decide on lawn irrigation as part of your plan. An in-ground sprinkler system is a big investment, but if it's the best option for you, do it early in whatever plan you have for the lawn. You don't want to be undertaking major modifications after renovating an older lawn or planting a new lawn. Add the list of all the changes you want to make to the sketch you've created. Lastly, you'll want to schedule those changes, including a calendar of the maintenance your lawn will require.

A plush, perfect lawn like this one is the result of careful feeding, meticulous watering, and mowing to ideal height for the grass species. All should be elements of any lawn-care plan.

Scheduling Lawn Care

Lawn maintenance, such as fertilizing and mowing, needs to be done on a schedule. Trying to make up for lost time inevitably leads to lawn damage and problems such as fertilizer burn. Lawn care done in a timely fashion, and according to the timetable that is best for your particular species of grass, ultimately means less effort and trouble in the long run.

A simple lawn-care schedule is an incredibly useful tool in helping you keep on top of your lawn's health. The schedule shown here lists the basic maintenance chores for both warm- and cold-season lawns, but you'll need to add to or change the schedule to accommodate the needs of your own particular grass, the variations in your local climate, and your personal preferences.

This schedule is also limited to those general chores that are done on a yearly basis. You should plan on testing your soil every two or three years. You'll also need to leave time to aerate and dethatch as necessary.

COOL-SEASON	WARM-SEASON
January–March	Protect the lawn from damage such as foot traffic and salt overspray. Continue mowing regularly if your lawn has not gone dormant, water during hot spells
April	Treat for crabgrass where applicable; rake up yard debris; tune up and sharpen lawn mower and prep other power equipment; begin mowing as the grass begins to grow; begin regular weeding. Add amendments as necessary
May	Topdress with compost or similar amendment if treating naturally; apply grub control as necessary; fertilize. Raise mowing height except on Bermuda grass; inspect for early insect outbreaks
June–August	Mow until lawn goes dormant; water regularly to supply amount necessary for your grass type; watch for insect outbreaks and infestation; fertilize cool season grasses in late August, just as weather cools, possibly with weed control. Mow as often as necessary to ensure lawn is kept at ideal height; fertilize warm season grasses midsummer; check for insect outbreaks and treat as necessary
September–October	Continue mowing as long as grass is actively growing, but lower the mowing height by ½"; reduce watering slightly. Watch for disease outbreaks, fertilize as necessary, overseed with cool-season grass seed as preferred
November–December	Winterize mower and power equipment for storage over winter months. Remove leaves and debris off lawn as necessary; check for fall insect outbreaks

Planning for Organic Lawn Care ▸

Choosing to grow an organic or natural lawn is actually a pretty significant commitment. Transitioning your lawn from chemical food, weed, disease, and pest controls to more natural solutions can easily take a year or more, and will inevitably mean more effort on your part up front. (There's a reason people commonly use powerful chemicals: they're easy and quick.)

Before you jump in with both feet, it helps to know the terminology. Organic and natural are often confused because the difference between the two is subtle. Generally, and for the purposes of this book, natural lawn care relates to preferring natural processes and products, even if they may have been exposed to synthetic materials. Organic is strictly non-chemical, and true organic lawn-care professionals won't even use compost made from organic materials that may have been exposed to chemicals.

Generally, organic proponents believe that treating the lawn with chemicals for whatever reason—fertilizing, fighting weeds, or even battling diseases—creates as many problems as it solves, because chemical treatments tend to kill the good with the bad. They also feel that the introduction of chemicals to moderate what are natural processes damages the environment at large and the health of individuals who come in contact with those chemicals.

THE ORGANIC PROCESS

Organic lawn care is a philosophy that makes very different assumptions than would be the norm in traditional lawn care. For instance, an organic groundskeeper assumes that some weeds in the lawn are not necessarily a problem, and may even be a good thing. The common white clover that so many homeowners fight hard to get rid of is considered a boon to most organic proponents, for its nitrogen-fixing and year-round greenery (not to mention the lovely white flowers). Organic enthusiasts also believe the way to help a lawn survive drought, disease, and other stressful conditions is to reinforce the lawn's own natural defenses.

STRIKING A BALANCE

If a grass-only lawn is your goal, taking care of the lawn in a truly organic way requires a lot of work. You'll either have to set up a compost bin and begin using it, or you'll need to purchase a lot of compost. You'll also be weeding by hand when you need to, and checking the amount of water your lawn consumes much more closely, as well as testing your soil on a regular basis.

But don't feel bad if you can't find the time or energy to brew your own compost tea. Look at the transition as an incremental process; it doesn't happen overnight. And, in fact, many people would say that even if you don't

An organic lawn-care proponent is willing to overlook (and may welcome) a scattering of clover in the lawn. You might find that from a distance, having a few beneficial plants among the grass in your lawn doesn't appreciably detract from the appearance.

change your ways to conform to completely organic lawn care methods, any change at all is a change in the right direction. The first step you might want to take is smart shopping. When comparing lawn-care products, look for the Organic Materials Review Institute label. The institute is a non-profit organization that evaluates different products that are produced and labeled as "organic." In a sense, the OMRI unofficially certifies products as organic. So picking products with the OMRI label will ensure that you're at least buying organic.

Keep in mind that some organic practices, such as mowing the lawn high to conserve water and spur root development, and allowing clippings to remain on the lawn, may ultimately reduce the amount of work you need to do in maintaining your lawn.

Then, whenever you can, begin to institute organic or natural practices. Buying a compost bin and using it is a great start, but you might also think about removing weeds manually rather than using a synthetic herbicide (look at it as extra exercise), and mowing your lawn slightly higher to conserve water and improve the health of the grass.

Who knows? Eventually you may catch the bug and begin brewing your own compost tea after all!

THINKING GREEN WITH THE HELP OF THE GOVERNMENT

Greenscaping is a philosophy that is promoted by the Environmental Protection Agency (EPA) as a way to conserve resources and preserve the outdoor areas of our homes. Greenscaping focuses on five steps: Building and maintaining healthy soil; planting right for your site; practicing smart watering; adopting a holistic approach to pest management; and practicing natural lawn care. The program focuses on reducing waste and the amount of chemicals you introduce into your lawn, as well as reducing the amount of pollutants you introduce into the environment by using manual lawn-care equipment. Key to greenscaping is the idea of reusing clippings and organic wastes in the form of compost, and recycling water, including rainwater and gray water. Lastly, the EPA recommends "rebuying"—the practice of purchasing goods that are all or part recycled materials. As with the practice of organic lawn care at large, the idea is to embrace as much of the greenscaping philosophy as you reasonably and practically can. To learn more, go to www.epa.com, or visit your local cooperative extension office.

Look for the OMRI label for assurance that products are organic.

Renewing an Older Lawn

Perhaps you inherited a lawn that hasn't seen the best of care (sellers are often more worried about their next house than keeping their current lawn in the peak of health). Or it might be that nature just got ahead of you. If your lawn has seen better days and is beyond the help of a little extra watering, a quick mow, and a dose of fertilizer, it may well be time to completely renew it.

Even if you've taken reasonably good care of your lawn, soil can fatigue and the lawn itself can become stressed enough that it can't rebound to full health. In this case, you'll need to take action. That usually means starting with a good dethatching to clear out the dead growth that is preventing nutrients from getting to the soil, which in turn prevents healthy new grass growth. You'll also need to introduce more air and organic material into the soil in a process known as *aerating*. And you might as well take the time to correct minor problems in the structure of the lawn, such as depressions or areas where the mower has repeatedly scalped the lawn.

Fortunately, lawns are fairly resilient. With a little time and elbow grease, you can return your front or backyard lawn to dense, deep green brilliance.

In this chapter:

- Renew or Replace?
- Dealing With Thatch
- Dethatching Your Lawn
- Aerating Your Lawn
- Leveling the Lawn Surface
- Repairing Bare Spots
- Overseeding

Renew or Replace?

The first step in renewing a tired lawn is determining if it is worth renewing, or if you'd be better served by starting over with a brand new lawn. A complete lawn rehabilitation will take significant work and a bit of expense. You'll also need to be patient while your front yard or backyard looks ratty in the short term, so that you can have a magnificent lawn down the road. Obviously, nobody wants to make that investment if the chances of success are slim.

There are certain criteria that will help you decide the best course of action. The first of these is just a matter of how much grass is left in your lawn. If actual grass plants make up less than 50 percent of the lawn, you're wiser to shut it down, kill everything and start with new sod or seed.

If, on the other hand, the lawn is still mostly grass, you need to figure out how many problems you'll have to deal with in renewing it. A wide range of troubles indicates lawn and soil that has been fundamentally compromised. For instance, if weeds are your main concern, there are a number of ways to eradicate them while strengthening the lawn to protect against any re-emergence. The solution is to eradicate the weeds, and take measures such as aeration to help the lawn grow stronger. A pretty easy fix, all in all.

But the more problems you add, the harder any fix becomes. Say you have all those weeds to deal with, but there are also signs of grub infestation, several areas of dollar spot disease, obvious soil compaction, and grass color that indicates a deficiency of nutrients. In that case, it's simply going to be easier to start over with freshly amended soil and a new lawn, than it would be to do everything necessary to deal with all the problems. Not to mention, the more problems your lawn has, the less chance of success any rehabilitation effort has.

Some localized problems, such as that awful path through the center of lawn from where the kids run back and forth to the back door, may look really bad. But in most cases, these specific issues are actually quite simple to deal with.

When all signs point to renewing the lawn, it's time to dive in and remove the thatch, get air to the root system, fix bare spots and bumps, feed and water, and return your lawn to the magnificent centerpiece of your yard that it was meant to be.

Multiple deficiencies affect most lawns. Choosing how to deal with them amounts to deciding if your current yard is worth saving. A thorough aeration and seeding can bring some lawns roaring back to life. But whether you choose to save it or scrap it (and this lawn is probably salvageable), make sure you address the source of any problems. For example, create a designated area for your dog to relieve himself.

A lawn that has surrendered this much territory to aggressive weeds is done for. Although you could apply a selective herbicide, any attempt to eliminate this level of weed infestation would be long-term, intensive and probably doomed to failure. Unfortunately, the answer here is to use a non-selective herbicide to kill everything (or solarize the field if you want to go the environmentally responsible route) and start fresh.

Large patches of bare ground surrounded by comparatively healthy turfgrass probably means you have a plant disease that requires treatment as part of your lawn renovation or replacement project.

Dealing With Thatch

Thatch is proof that too much of a good thing is a bad thing. Normal thatch is a valuable layer of decomposing organic material that settles around the base of your grass plants. A modest amount of thatch creates a protective layer over the soil, helping retain moisture, and it breaks down over time into necessary nutrients. Thatch isn't a problem until it builds up and becomes thicker than a half inch.

Once the thatch is too thick, you need to do something about it: it prevents water, fertilizer, lawn seed, and beneficial organic material from reaching the soil. A thick layer of thatch will essentially starve the grass roots and dry out the soil. It also provides an excellent breeding ground for unwanted insects and disease. In other words, a thick layer of thatch is a gateway for trouble.

Thatch buildup itself can be a symptom of other problems. Normally, the organic material that comprises thatch is food for beneficial microorganisms and desirable soil life such as earthworms, which keep it from collecting in mass. Excess thatch is a sign that those organisms are not on the job, which can mean that something, such as an excessive application of fertilizer, has killed them off. A deep layer of thatch can also mean

that you're cutting off too much of the grass when you mow. Longer clippings take longer to decompose.

The best way to handle thatch is to physically remove it on a regular schedule, so it does not get out of control. A deep, vigorous yearly raking with a bamboo or steel-tined leaf rake (plastic tines generally don't do the job as well) will go a long way toward preventing any serious thatch buildup. Just be sure to remove the debris you pull up—it makes excellent fuel for a compost pile. You'll want to be especially vigilant if you live in a southern state. Warm-season grasses are more likely to develop excessive thatch buildup than cool-season grasses are, because warm-season species actively grow over a longer period.

The next line of defense is lawn aeration (see page 55). This can be done on a small lawn with a manual aerator, or it you can use a rented power core aerator if your yard is larger. Either way, the idea is to punch holes through the layer of thatch at the same time as you are punching holes in the soil. Aeration usually works best for thatch layers that are no thicker than ¾ inch. Once the thatch exceeds 1 inch thick, you'll be faced with the more involved process of dethatching the entire lawn.

Beat Thatch Buildup ▶

Some simple maintenance practices can help you keep thatch to a minimum and prevent buildup from becoming a problem.

- Mow frequently. Cut less than ⅓ of the blade length each time you mow and the clippings are less likely to pile up.
- Mulch when you mow. Using a mulching mower will cut the clippings even finer, ensuring they break down and disintegrate as quickly as possible.

- Fertilize sparingly. One of the most common mistakes homeowners make is fertilizing too much, or too much at one time. Explosive growth contributes to buildup of thatch, so it's better to go a little light on the fertilizer application.
- Water deeply. Frequent shallow waterings causes root systems and organic matter to cluster close to the surface. The deeper you water, the further down your lawn's roots will grow, and the less thatch will accumulate.

Dethatching Your Lawn

When it becomes clear that a deep raking or a simple aeration isn't going to solve your thatch buildup, it's time to undertake a real dethatching. But be aware that dethatching seriously stresses your lawn, chewing up your soil and damaging grass blades and crowns. Be careful not to do more harm than good.

Although you can dethatch with a special tool called a cavex rake, the process is fairly laborious when done by hand. It makes more sense—even for an average size yard—to rent a power dethatcher. These machines are usually called vertical mowers due to the orientation of their blades. They are extremely effective at digging out thick layers of thatch. They are also easy to use, and are similar in operation to a gas-powered lawn mower. You'll find them in the lineup at most equipment rental outlets.

Perhaps the most important part of using a vertical mower is setting the blades to the proper cutting depth so they remove thatch without cutting too deep into your soil. Start with a setting between ⅛ and ¼ inch, going deeper if needed to remove all the thatch.

The time that you select to remove the thatch is just as important as how you go about it. You should dethatch cool-season lawns in mid to late summer, right before they green up in fall. Warm-season lawns are best dethatched in late winter or early spring, before they start their summer growth spurt. The idea is to put the lawn through the trauma of dethatching right before it goes into a period of active growth, when it will best be able to recover. For the same reason, lightly fertilize and water thoroughly right after you finish dethatching.

If your thatch buildup is more than 1½ inches, don't remove all of it at once. Run the machine once each way and then wait until the lawn recovers before dethatching again. A few basic practices will ensure that you minimize the trauma of dethatching and help the lawn rebound effectively to grow even stronger after the process has been completed.

- Avoid feeding the lawn. If you're planning on dethatching, don't fertilize for at least two months before you do it. The same goes for treating the lawn with any kind of preemergence weedkiller. Wait until right after you've dethatched the lawn.
- Water the lawn lightly before dethatching, or dethatch it right after a light rain. The soil should be moist, but not sodden or bone dry.
- Mow low. Cut the lawn below the minimum of the recommend height for your species. Bag or rake all the clippings off the lawn.
- Always start power dethatching with the machine set high. You can then lower the blades to remove all the thatch after you become used to its operation.
- Water deeply as soon as you're done.

A vertical mower (also called a power rake) makes quick work of the rigorous job of dethatching your lawn.

How to Use a Vertical Mower

Use marking paint to mark all underground lines and cables, including utility, power, and gas lines, and television cables. Mark in-ground sprinkler lines and head locations.

Mow the lawn to about half the height you would normally mow it, bagging the clippings. Rake up any leaves and debris on the surface of the lawn.

Adjust the vertical mower to the correct depth for your grass (the rental store can advise you on how to do this). Make the first pass, and adjust the settings as necessary.

Warning ▶

For the most part, vertical mowers are easy to use because they are operated much like a walk-behind mower. But don't let their similarity to mowers allow you to forget that they are dangerous power equipment capable of causing injury (as well as causing damage to your yard if used improperly). Always wear safety glasses, sturdy shoes or boots, and long pants. Don't ever turn the unit on its side when it is running. If it binds up or catches debris, shut it off and then inspect under the deck.

- Be aware that there are many different blade designs for vertical mowers. When renting one, never leave the rental center until you are absolutely clear on how to adjust, change, or set the blades for the particular machine you'll be using. The rental center pro should brief you on this and other safety issues.

Make the second pass at a 90° angle to the first, and alternate in this way until you've covered the entire lawn.

Rake up the waste left behind by the vertical mower. Compost this debris unless you have previously treated the lawn with chemicals.

Thinking Green ▶

You can avoid the use of a gas-guzzling machine by dethatching your lawn manually. All the process requires is a special implement called a *cavex* rake and lots of elbow grease (look at it as a chance to get some exercise while improving your lawn and the air quality). This rake is equipped with sharp, crescent-shaped blades. To use the rake, force it down and pull hard to cut smoothly through the thatch, removing it as you pull. Collect and compost the debris you remove after you're done.

Cavex rakes are typically used on smaller plots of grass because they require a lot of effort, but regardless of where you use one, rake over a given area of grass only once. First-time users have a tendency to overuse with a cavex rake, which can stress the grass.

Aerating Your Lawn

Living creatures need air, and the roots of your turfgrass plants are no different. Unfortunately, soil can become compacted over time, making it too dense to effectively allow air, water, and nutrients to reach grass roots. Compacted soil slows and can even stop grass from growing.

Aeration—the process of creating openings in the soil structure—is the cure for compaction. It literally opens up the soil, bringing essential air and water to the roots, while allowing those roots a loose structure through which to spread. Aerating your lawn prevents thatch buildup (and can alleviate an existing thatch problem), ensures that fertilizer finds its way deep into the soil rather than languishing on top, and generally creates a very hospitable environment for beneficial microorganisms.

The aeration process is simple. It involves pulling cores of soil out of the ground and depositing them on top, where they will dry out and break up naturally. The holes left behind are made at regular intervals about 3" apart.

You can use any of a number of manual aerators available on the market, but the most effective and quickest way to aerate is to rent a power core aerator. This machine features rows of hollow tines on a roller or other device. As you move it forward, the tines jab down into the soil about 3" deep, pulling up cores and ejecting them onto the lawn.

No matter which kind of aerator you use, be sure that the soil is slightly moist; if it's too wet, it will bog down the machine or manual aerator, and mud will fill in the holes. If it's too dry, you'll have a very rough go of it as the machine struggles to penetrate the surface.

You'll also need to plan the right time for aeration. Cool-season lawns should be aerated in late summer to early fall, while warm-season lawns are aerated in late spring. Adjust this time a bit to ensure that you don't aerate during the germination period for weeds common to your area. Because it's gentler on the lawn than dethatching, you can aerate once a year. Follow up aeration with a topdressing of compost or other organic amendment to get the most out of the process. Water deeply after you're done. Post-aeration is also a good time to overseed the lawn and feed it with a light application of fertilizer.

The Compaction Test ▸

You can determine if your lawn is a candidate for aeration with a very simple test. Try sticking the point of a long Phillips head screwdriver into your soil. If you have a hard time pushing it in, it's a good sign that the lawn is overdue for aeration.

Power aerating your lawn creates openings for air and nutrients to get deep into the root system. It also creates hundreds of dirt cylinders that can be left to dry and then worked back in.

How to Use a Power Core Aerator

Water the entire yard lightly a few hours before you aerate to ensure that the soil is moist—but don't overwater or you will bog down the machine in mud.

Flag all sprinkler heads, shallow sprinkler lines and shallow buried cables, wires and utility lines. Clear the lawn of other debris such as small tree branches.

Set the depth gauge on the coring machine to maximum. Run the machine across the lawn, back and forth in one direction. Then run it again, perpendicular to the original direction.

Allow the cores pulled up by the aerator to dry for a day, then gently rake across them to break them up so that they decompose more quickly.

Leveling the Lawn Surface

Over time, the topography of a lawn changes. Tree roots grow, then die and decay. Certain areas of the lawn settle more than others. Burrowing rodents leave behind tunnels long after you get rid of the pests. Simple erosion sometimes takes its toll. All that can add up to an uneven lawn surface, and an uneven lawn surface creates potential problems.

Even a minor hump in the lawn can lead to scalping during mowing, creating an unattractive bare spot. A depression in the lawn can collect water and organic debris, becoming an entry point for pests and diseases that can end up affecting the whole lawn. An uneven surface makes the lawn far less usable for play and recreation and, depending on how deep or high the irregularities are, detracts from the look of your lawn. Given how easy lawn high and low points are to fix, there's just no reason to tolerate them. Basically, all you'll need is about half an hour, a half-moon edger, a

trowel, and a bucket full of topsoil or "black dirt" with sand in it.

Leveling the lawn is most logically done as part of an overall lawn renovation, and is the perfect follow-up to lawn dethatching and aeration. But if it works better for your schedule, there's no reason you can't do it at other times. Just be sure to remedy the initial cause of the dip or bulge before you level the area.

Tools & Materials ▸

Half-moon edger
Flat garden spade
Garden rake
Gloves

Non-hydrated lime
  or landscape
  marking paint
Topsoil or horticultural soil

How to Level High and Low Spots

Clearly identify the area to be raised or lowered, by marking the perimeter with sprinkled non-hydrated lime. Cut the edges with a half-moon edger or garden spade, then use a flat spade to cut roots a few inches under the turf.

Remove the sod over the repair area. Set it aside and moisten it before continuing with the repair.

**Handy Fix
for Little Dips ▸**

You can use a groundskeeper's
shortcut to fill in shallow
depressions in the lawn.
Simply cover the depression
with a light topping of potting
soil and water. The soil will
sift down and the grass will
eventually grow on top of
it. Do this regularly until the
depression is leveled out.

Fill the depression with topsoil—or remove soil to level a bump—until it's level
with the surrounding soil. Smooth off the top surface and lightly tamp down the soil.

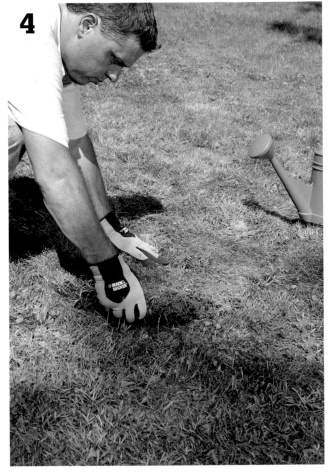

Water the repair area, just until the soil is moist. Replace
the sod patch you cut out, being sure to position it in its
original orientation.

Step on the turf over the repair or use the back of a
steel-tined rake to seat the sod and ensure the turf is in solid
contact with the soil. Water the repair area well.

Repairing Bare Spots

Bare spots are one of the most common afflictions in older lawns. Over time, foot traffic tends to follow the same path, wearing out the grass and compacting the soil in particular spots. Pets are also creatures of habit and they tend to do their business in the same place repeatedly. Certain diseases can also lead to a bald patch, as can incidental trauma, such as a burn from spilled fertilizer or gasoline. With so many potential causes, it's a wonder that more lawns aren't suffering from bare spots!

Fixing these eyesores begins with solving whatever the cause might be (for solutions to individual problems, see The Lawn Problem-Solving Guide, pages 158–159). Then it's just a matter of bringing life back to the area, a process that is helped by the lawn growth around the patch. Create a favorable environment with seed or sod, and the surrounding grass will look to move in as well.

Patching bare spots works best if you do it at the beginning of new lawn growth. Repair bare spots in the late summer for cool-season grasses, and in late spring for warm-season species. Either way, always water well whether you're planting sod or seed. Every day for a week is a good baseline (if there has been no rain) and continue watering until you're sure the patch is completely established.

Tools & Materials ▸

Garden spade	Metal tamper
Garden fork	or 4 × 4 scrap
Garden rake	Grass seed
Large, sharp knife	Compost
Sod	Starter fertilizer

Bare spots are not only unsightly, they can spread if the primary cause is left untreated. They are entry points for other problems such as lawn diseases.

How to Patch a Bare Spot With Sod

Use a spade to cut a square or rectangle shape around the damaged or bare patch. This will make it easier to snugly fit the sod patch in place.

Break up the soil with a garden fork and mix in compost or a similar amendment. Level the patch area to about 1" below the surrounding turf. Lightly tamp the soil down with a scrap 4 × 4 or metal tamper.

Measure the patch area and cut a piece of sod to fit snugly. It's better to cut it slightly larger and then trim it to fit as necessary. Use a large, sharp knife to cut the sod.

Settle the patch with the back of a garden rake to ensure good contact with the soil below. Water well, keeping the patch moist until it is well established.

How to Patch a Bare Spot With Seed/Fertilizer Mix

Rake out dead grass or other debris. Use a garden fork to break up the soil. Rake and moisten the prepared area.

Add combination seed and fertilizer mix to the soil within the borders of the bare spot. Spread at the rate recommended on the package. Feather the mixture outside of he borders slightly to help it blend in with the surrounding turf.

Use the top of the rake to level the patch area even with the surrounding soil surface, raking the amended mix out from the edges of the patch as necessary. Water the patched areas thoroughly and continue to water regularly and deeply until the new grass plants are well established.

The Premixed Solution ▸

Seeding a bare spot requires a lot of follow up, primarily to ensure that the seeds and seedlings are kept moist until established, and that birds and other wildlife don't poach the seed. An alternative—involving slightly more money and slightly less effort—is a lawn patch mix. These all-in-one products combine seed, a binder such as ground-up paper mixed with gel, and a starter fertilizer. Simply spread the mix over the bare spot after you've prepared the surface, and water regularly (some mixes don't even require watering) until the new grass takes root.

How to Patch a Dead Spot With Seed

Identify the type of grass surrounding the dead spot or bare spot. If your local lawn and garden center carries a combination seed/fertilizer mixture containing that type of seed, use it (see previous page). If not, locate plain grass seed of that type from the store or a seed catalog.

Dig out the dead spot or remove a thin layer of dirt from the bare spot. Add a layer of compost or topsoil/compost mixture to the repair area so the top is slightly above the dirt level surrounding it.

Scatter the seed over the repair area, following the coverage rate recommended by the seed package. Spread a thin layer of compost over the seed. Correct compost coverage leaves some of the seed still visible. Water thoroughly.

Protect the repair area by staking it out with stakes and caution tape. Continue watering with the stakes in place until the new grass plants are well established.

Overseeding

Overseeding is the practice of spreading new seed over an existing lawn. It is perhaps the most underappreciated and underused lawn-care technique. That's especially true when it comes to renovating an existing, older lawn. It's simply plain science: grass plants literally "tire" after half a dozen years or so. Their growth slows, making an older lawn susceptible to thinning. With thinning comes many other problems.

The way to fight thinning and keep your lawn as dense as brand-new sod, is to properly overseed the lawn on a regular basis (once every few years should do it). The benefit is twofold. First, you get a lawn that is as lush as the day it was laid (or when it first filled in). Second, and more important, dense new grass growth crowds out weeds.

There's another benefit as well: Seed companies are constantly developing new, stronger, more disease-resistant grass varieties. By overseeding, you take advantage of these developments because you're introducing the latest grass types.

The best time to overseed for cool-season lawns is in early fall, while the optimum time for warm-season grass is in early spring. Either way, the actual process is a fairly simple one.

Start by raking the lawn. Don't be gentle; you're trying to remove all the organic debris lying on top of the soil that might prevent seeds from reaching it, while scratching the surface to prepare for the new seed. Now mow about half the height you normally would (you may have already done this as part of a general lawn renovation). Collect the

To help seeds sprout after overseeding, cover them with a thin layer of compost or topsoil mix spread with the spreader, just as you did with the seeds.

clippings in a bag or, if your mower doesn't have a bag attachment, you'll need to rake them up. In any case, a second raking perpendicular to the direction you used the first time is a good idea to thoroughly prep the soil. If you were planning on topdressing the lawn, now is the time to do it. Then it's time to start overseeding.

Spread seed with a broadcast or drop spreader. Seed bags or boxes list the spreader rate for both new lawns and overseeding. You can use the company's recommendations or, as many professionals do, use the setting for seeding new lawns when you're overseeding. This gives you a better shot at success because, depending on your local climate and conditions, as few as half of the seeds you spread may actually germinate and grow.

Spread seed in the same way you spread fertilizer. Walk in rows at an appropriate pace that maintains the correct spreading rate, and overlap rows by a couple of inches. It's always a good idea to practice first on a hard surface such as a driveway, to get the proper pacing down.

A modest application of a starter fertilizer will improve the chances that a majority of the seeds establish themselves and grow. You can also topdress with a little compost as a protective cover for the seeds. Some professionals follow up a month later with an application of quick-release nitrogen fertilizer to turbocharge seedling growth.

One of the keys to overseeding success is to keep the new seeds moist. You don't want them to drown, but they shouldn't ever dry out. This usually means watering every day that it doesn't rain, and twice a day in very hot weather. You should also take precautions to keep people, pets, and other traffic off the lawn until the seedlings are completely established.

Protecting Your Seeds ▸

Birds consider overseeding a catered meal. Exposed seeds are likely to get eaten and even if they don't, grass seeds are fairly fragile. Too much heat, too little water or even a stiff wind can prevent them from germinating and filling out your lawn. To help overseeding pay off, consider protecting seeds and seedlings with special fabric manufactured for this purpose. Called "all-purpose garden fabric", this is available through home centers, nurseries and garden supply outlets. Simply lay it on top of the newly seeded lawn and keep it moist—birds and the elements will effectively be blocked from getting to the seeds. Be aware, though, that this type of fabric should only be used in cool weather. The fabric traps heat and can smother the seeds in hot weather.

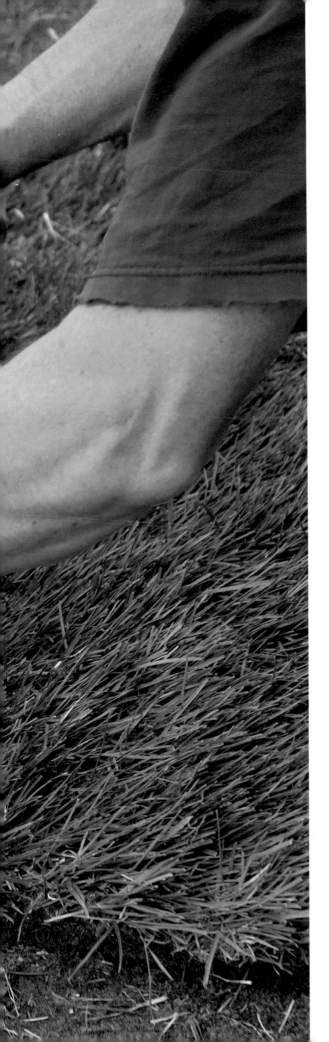

Planting a New Lawn

There are several reasons you might want to plant a new lawn. In some cases, your old lawn is beyond the point of rescue. Or you may be moving into a newly built house. In some instances, you simply want to convert an unattractive yard feature, such as a parking area, into a luxuriant, living surface.

Planting a new lawn is one home improvement project that offers a big reward provided that you do not skimp on planning and preparation. Given the time, effort, and money you'll need to put toward your new lawn, it simply doesn't make sense to take shortcuts. You should thoroughly improve your soil as much as possible, take all necessary steps to prevent weeds in your new lawn, and choose just the right time to actually plant or seed the lawn. This is also the perfect time to install an in-ground sprinkler system.

Aside from proper preparation, you'll need to decide whether you'll be using sod, plugs, or seeds to start your new lawn. Each has its own pros and cons, but basically the more expensive the option, the less time you'll have to wait for a rich, mature lawn.

In this chapter:

- New Lawn Options
- Selecting Sod
- Selecting Grass Seed
- Selecting Lawn Plugs
- Removing an Old Lawn
- Preparing Your Soil
- Adding Topsoil
- Amending Soil With Compost
- Natural Soil Amendments
- Maintaining Proper Soil pH
- Grading for Proper Drainage
- Laying Sod
- Planting a Lawn From Seed

New Lawn Options

Once you've decided to plant a new lawn, you'll choose between three options: sod, seeds, or plugs. Your choice should be driven by a combination of how much you're willing to spend, the specific conditions of your yard, and how quickly you want to see the results of your efforts. Balance the relative importance of each to determine which method is right for you, your budget, and your yard.

Expense is, as always, a crucial factor. The larger the lawn, the more you'll feel the difference when you write the check. Laying a lawn of sod is about 20 times more expensive than growing that same lawn from seed, and about 10 times more expensive than planting plugs. You can expect sod costs to average around 25 cents per square foot. This cost will vary depending on a number of factors, including what grass species you're buying and how far you are from the sod farm. But that extra money buys you a couple of key advantages. The first is flexible timing. Sod can be laid at just about any time of the year, although the hotter it is, the more of a challenge you'll face in getting the sod safely laid, rooted, and established. In contrast, seeded or plugged lawns are only planted in early fall for cold-season varieties, and mid to late spring for warm-season grasses. If you absolutely have to have a lawn in the middle of summer for your daughter's wedding reception, sod would be the way to go.

The other major benefit to sod is instant gratification. A lawn of reasonable size can be laid with sod in less than a day. In a week, you'll be able to walk on it, and in two weeks it will be hard to tell the difference from a year-old lawn. Lawns grown from seed, on the other hand, will take weeks to establish and a month or more to become as lush and verdant as a sodded lawn is the day after it's laid. Plugs are an odd man out, because they look lush where there's grass, but it may take two full growing seasons to fully fill in the entire lawn area.

The terrain of your yard may also play a part in your decision. For instance if your lawn will be situated on a steep slope, you'd be wise to consider sod or plugs because seeds are likely to wash away during watering or rain. Laying sod is more work than spreading seed, and plugging a lawn is more laborious still. There are, however, many more species available in seed form than in sod.

Sometimes, the only remedy for a failing lawn is to replace it. Whether you choose seeds, sod, or plugs to create your new lawn, the key to success is in the preparation of the soil base and, in three simple words: water, water, water.

Selecting Sod

The relatively high price of sod is due to the fact that someone is growing your lawn for you. That someone is a sod farmer, who literally grows acres and acres of turfgrass. When he receives an order, the farmer goes out into the field and cuts the number of square feet you need of the grass species you want. Sod farmers cut to a standardized width of 2 feet, in lengths ranging from 6 to 8 feet long. They cut the sod 2 to 3 inches deep, depending on the variety.

Once cut, the sections of sod are folded or rolled, and stacked on pallets for shipping to the client. That signals that the clock is ticking. The longer the sod takes to get where it's ultimately going, the worse condition it will be in when it gets there. Ideally, you want to receive your sod within a day or two of it being cut.

The problem is, even when kept moist, that sod is not getting the proper nutrients. After about four days, the grass will start to show signs of damage, and will be somewhat less likely to root as completely and strongly as new sod would. So the point is, do whatever it takes to get the sod delivered as quickly as possible after it's been cut. Most homeowners buy sod through a third-party nursery or garden center, and it's wise to ask questions—especially about how long after cutting the sod will take to reach you. Be your own advocate, and if you don't like the answers you're getting, move on to another supplier (most suppliers in the areas share sod farms, but not all will have the same relationship with the farmer).

When ordering sod, you'll need to calculate the square footage of your yard. That's pretty simple if it's a square or rectangle, but can be a bit of a challenge if the lawn area is an irregular shape with odd areas that are hard to accurately measure. When ordering for a basic geometric shape, add 10 percent to account for waste or measuring mistakes. If your yard is an unusual shape, allow yourself a 15- to 20-percent buffer to be safe.

The best sod is the freshest. Always ask how long the sod will sit after cutting and before it's transported to your site.

Selecting Grass Seed

The last decade has seen amazing advances in the science of turfgrass seeds. New varieties are stronger, more insect- and disease-resistant, and able to tolerate much greater stress than earlier types. Spend the time and attention to select the right seeds for your lawn and they will pay off not only in how well the lawn does in the short term, but also how gracefully and trouble-free it ages.

To start with, you'll be choosing between a blend or mix of seeds. Seeds are rarely sold as just one varietal of one species because mixing seed to one degree or another generally creates a stronger lawn overall. Whenever possible though, look for a mixture rather than a blend. A blend combines different species that may or may not work well in your given location and conditions. A mixture is different varieties of the same species, and works especially well in fighting diseases, weeds, and

pests common to that species. Mixtures are more common among warm-season grasses; if you live in a colder part of the country blends may be your only option. Most blends also include what are called "nurse grasses," species or varieties that grow quickly and provide a good environment for the rest of the seeds in the mix. No matter which you buy, consult your local cooperative extension office for recommendations of grass species and varieties that do well in your area.

You'll also have to determine how much seed to buy. Take an accurate measurement of the square footage of your lawn and check that measurement against the coverage recommendations listed on the box or bag. Purchase more seed than you need because the extra can come in handy for reseeding troublespots or overseeding in the future.

The Story on the Label ▸

Grass seed boxes and bags are required by law to clearly list detailed information about the ingredients on the label. Consequently, the label is the first place to look when shopping for seed. The variety or species in the mix are listed by their "purity" or the percentage of each that makes up the total bag contents. You'll also find a germination rate that tells you what percentage of each type of seed can be expected to sprout and grow into a grass plant. Surprisingly, you'll also find a percentage of weed seed in the mix. This is because it's difficult to cultivate and harvest grass seed without collecting some weed seeds—and it's even harder to "clean" the mix and remove those seeds. Ideally, this number should be 0, but a weed seed percentage of less than .5 is considered acceptable (the higher the percentage, the poorer quality of the mix in general). Inert matter, or filler, is also listed. Although this doesn't usually affect how successful the seed mix or blend will be, you want the numbers close to 0. Read the label carefully and with a critical eye, and you'll wind up with a seed product that spells success for your new lawn.

A grass mixture contains different varieties of the same species, whereas a blend contains seeds from multiple turfgrass species.

Selecting Lawn Plugs

Growing a lawn from plugs falls in the middle ground between seeding and sodding a lawn. The plugs are cut from sod in 2- to 4-inches squares (or, less often, rounds), which are then planted individually in a grid across the lawn's area. The cost is a little over half of what sod would run you to cover the same area, but is still 10 times more expensive than seed.

Labor-wise, planting plugs is on par with the effort you'd dedicate to laying sod, because each plug is planted in an individual hole. The plugs are purchased in much the same way as sod is, through a nursery or garden center that contracts with a grower.

The grower cuts the plugs from sod, and so can you. But that will double your workload, without saving you much money. Buying plugs is, therefore, usually the wiser course of action. But use the same criteria for plugs that you would for assessing the quality of sod. You want them as fresh as possible, kept moist and cool.

Be aware that depending on the type of grass, plugs can take up to two growing seasons to completely fill in a lawn. In the interim, weeds are a big challenge for the bare spots between the plugs, and applying a selective herbicide is often part of the regular maintenance of a lawn grown from plugs. This drawback is the reason plugs are usually only offered for grasses that are prohibitively expensive as sod and those that aren't regularly available as seed. Zoysia is the most common grass planted from plugs for these reasons, and most plug grasses are warm-season species, because the longer growing cycle helps the lawn fill in quicker.

Plugs are small clumps of sod that are planted in a regular pattern as a cost-effective alternative to laying sod. It usually takes two growing seasons for the plug roots to entirely spread and fill out the lawn.

Removing an Old Lawn

Once you've decided that your current lawn is beyond reviving, you'll need to clear the field of old growth to give your new lawn the best possible chance to take hold and eventually thrive. Removing your old lawn is not difficult, but it will take a bit of labor. The amount of work you'll need to do depends on how much grass remains, but don't be tempted to just roto-till the old lawn under. That would be an invitation to weeds and disease to infiltrate the new grass.

Instead, take the time to kill all the plant life in the lawn with a general, non-selective herbicide (or use one of the natural solutions suggested below). Once all the plant life is dead, you'll need to completely remove it to prepare for the process of amending the soil. Keep in mind that non-selective herbicides can take two weeks to completely kill grass and weeds.

Tools & Materials ▸

Pump sprayer
Lawn mower
Sod cutter
Gloves

Square-edge shovel
  or spade
Non-selective herbicide

Thinking Green: Herbicide Alternatives ▸

Today's herbicides have been refined for minimal impact on humans and animals, while still effectively killing the plants you want to remove. However, overspray can harm other plant life in the yard and garden, and many people prefer to avoid using chemicals whenever possible. If you're focused on natural or organic solutions for the lawn, there are two highly effective alternatives to killing a worn-out lawn with herbicides.

Thick black plastic sheeting laid over the lawn creates an impermeable layer that kills everything underneath in about two weeks. This process is called solarizing because it amplifies the heat of the sun to kill most plant life under the plastic (many beneficial microorganisms and insects survive). Overlap rows and secure the sheeting with bricks or other weights. After solarizing, you should amend the soil with nutrients before planting the new lawn.

Newspaper laid down in thick layers over the lawn may be used instead of plastic. You'll need to spread a layer of mulch over the newspaper. Plan on one full growing season for this to be effective. The newspapers can also be composted after the growth underneath is completely dead.

"Solarizing" is the process of trapping heat underneath a dark membrane to kill plants in the topsoil. This method requires full sun.

How to Remove a Worn-Out Lawn

Prepare the lawn for spraying with a nonselective herbicide by watering deeply a week before you plan to spray. Choose a warm, calm day to spray. Mix a nonselective herbicide according to the directions and apply it to the entire lawn, avoiding any plants you don't wish to kill.

Allow at least two weeks for the plants to die and then scalp the lawn by setting a power mower to its lowest cutting height and then mowing the dead grass.

Options for Tilling Organic Material Into the Soil

Rent a powerful rear-tine rototiller and use it to break up the soil and dead grass, working the dead plant matter back into the soil. Make multiple passes to till down to a depth of 6".

Use a digging fork (resembles a pitchfork but with broader tines) to break up the soil and work the dead plant matter into the earth.

Preparing Your Soil

Whether you're planting sod, seed, or plugs, great soil preparation will be the difference between a good and a great lawn. Proper soil structure, nutrients and grading not only get your lawn off to a good start, they also go a long way toward heading off potential problems. Now—before the lawn is in place—is the best possible time to improve your soil. Without the top layer of growth, it's easy to make all the changes you need to create the perfect foundation for a brilliant lawn.

The first order of business is to amend the soil as necessary to improve the structure and add nutrients. You can use any amendments, but the best of these do double duty, improving structure and adding micro- and macronutrients. Turfgrasses prefer soil that allows air and nutrients to move down to and around the roots, but that doesn't drain so quickly that the roots don't have time to absorb them. The nutrients you need will be determined by the results of your soil test. But the beauty of most natural amendments is that the nutrients are slow-release. A healthy soil supports a broad range of beneficial organisms that will break down organic matter such as clippings, releasing essential nutrients in the process.

Amend the soil when it is just moist. The actual processes of amending and grading your soil are not complicated, requiring little more than hard effort with a shovel or a rototiller. But that elbow grease investment will pay off for as long as your lawn lives.

Tools & Materials ▸

Shovel	Leaf rake
Rototiller (optional)	Lawn roller
Wheelbarrow	Amendment
Garden rake	Starter fertilizer

Rototiller Wisdom ▸

Rototillers are amazing machines that can churn through soil like a hot knife through butter. Renting one for a day can cut hours and lots of labor off the chore of amending lawn soil. Tilling wet clay soil with a rototiller can actually harm soil structure, so wait until soil is just moist. Work the amendments about 6" into the soil. Finish by rolling the surface and you'll have set the stage for a healthy lawn. The light weight tiller shown here is useful for incorporating ammendments in soil that has already been broken with a fork or shovel. For breaking sod and compacted dirt, use a powerful rear-tine tiller or a tractor with a tiller attachment.

How to Prepare Soil for a New Lawn

Spread the amendments across the top of soil and use a shovel or rototiller to mix them in, digging down about 6" until the amendment is thoroughly mixed in.

Rake out the soil as level as possible, removing rocks or other large debris as you go. If you're installing sod, the level should be about 1" lower than surrounding areas, such as sidewalks or beds.

Apply the starter fertilizer appropriate for the grass you'll be planting, and water the soil so that it is thoroughly moist but still firm and not muddy.

Fill drum ¼-full only

Roll the soil with a light drum roller (fill a water-filled roller about ¼ full), to create a firm but not compacted surface for the seed or sod. Scratch the surface with a garden rake right before laying sod or seed.

Adding Topsoil

Topsoil is the rich base for your lawn, so the first order of business in making improvements is to ensure that there is actually enough topsoil in the first place. Although more is always better when it comes to topsoil, most gardeners agree that the topsoil under a lawn should be around 6" deep. If your topsoil is 4" or less, add a couple inches before laying or planting your lawn (keep in mind that sod brings with it about 1" of topsoil).

Purchase topsoil just as you do other amendments, by the cubic yard. Large garden centers and landscape supply outlets are some of the sources for topsoil. But regardless of where you purchase it, always ask where the topsoil came from. Home-building site excavations can be good sites for healthy topsoil, but excavated ditches along roads, and silt from waterbeds are not.

Inspect the topsoil before you buy. It should be a rich dark brown and somewhat moist. Good topsoil crumbles easily in your hand. The particles that comprise it should be of varying sizes, and the topsoil should be rich with decomposing humus. Horticultural soils are often sand-based, even though they are a rich black color. Also keep in mind that even after you've inspected it, it's never a bad idea to test the topsoil you're considering buying.

The new topsoil should be spread evenly across the surface of your yard and dug into the existing soil just as any other amendment would be. You can also use this opportunity to mix in compost or other amendments. Doing them all at the same time limits the amount of digging you'll need to do as well as any damage to the soil structure.

Ordering Topsoil ▶

Figuring out how much topsoil you need is just a matter of using a simple formula. It works like this:

Let's assume you want to add 3 inches of topsoil. If your yard is 1,000 square feet, begin calculating by starting with 1 foot of topsoil added to the yard. Because a cubic foot of new topsoil goes on top of each square foot of the yard, you would need 1,000 cubic feet of topsoil.

Now divide that figure by the number of cubic feet in a cubic yard (27). That gives you the number of cubic yards of topsoil you will need—37.

But since we actually want to add only 3 inches, and three is one-quarter of a foot, multiply the cubic yard number by .25.

Which gives the number of cubic yards you need: 9.25.

Because suppliers generally only sell in complete cubic yards, you'll buy 10.

High quality topsoil should be a rich, dark brown or black in color, with visible organic elements (humus). It should smell rich and earthy; a chemical smell or strong unpleasant odor is a sign of contaminated topsoil that is poorly suited to support healthy grass.

Amending Soil With Compost

Compost is one of the most common, useful, and potentially inexpensive amendments you can add to your soil. You can easily create your own compost, but given the amount that you will probably need to amend the soil in preparation for a new lawn, you'll most likely want to buy what you need from a local source. You can buy bagged compost, but that would be exceptionally pricey. It's wiser to buy in bulk, by the cubic yard.

Be aware that not all compost is created equal. Compost needs to be "finished" to be at its most useful; the compost itself should smell somewhat sweet. If it smells at all of ammonia, it's unfinished and you should find another source.

Good compost adds immeasurably to the soil. It improves the structure so that the soil drains well, but retains a good deal of moisture. Compost also adds a wealth of beneficial microorganisms to the soil (and often, larger helpers such as earthworms). The material is not as rich in nutrients as other amendments are. But although the amounts are lower, compost contains some amounts of all the macro- and micronutrients your lawn needs, in slow-release form. Use about three cubic yards for every 1,000 square feet of soil area.

Preparing for planting a new lawn is the perfect time to add compost to the soil, but it's not the only time. Compost is an excellent yearly top-dressing for a growing lawn, one that helps keep your soil healthy.

Thinking Green: Composting ▶

Making your own compost is a simple way to help the environment, help your lawn, and help yourself to one of the best soil improvements you can use.

Large home improvement stores and garden centers carry many different designs of composting bins, but all do the same basic things: contain the pile of yard and kitchen waste and other debris that you will be composting, provide for airflow around the pile, and allow access to remove the completed compost.

Of course, you can also make your own compost bin for free. Use scrap boards and posts to create a square bin, or chicken wire and poles to make a round one. You can even make a simple pile in an out-of-the way corner of the yard or garden.

Ultimately, how you maintain the pile is more important than the design of the composter. You'll be composting two types of organic materials, generally referred to as "browns" and "greens." Browns are leaves, twigs, bark, and dead flowers. Greens are grass clippings, kitchen waste, and other similar materials. To create the most efficient pile, use a ratio of two-to-one in favor of brown elements. Help a new pile get started with a compost starter kit available at nurseries and home centers.

Keep the pile moist, but not soaking wet. Turn it regularly; the more you turn it, the faster the materials will compost. You know the pile is working if the center is hot. Harvest it when the compost is finished. It should be black and crumbly with no recognizable bits or pieces of the original material.

Turning your compost regularly accelerates the conversion time it needs to be ready for your yard and garden.

Natural Soil Amendments

Add amendments to the soil with, or in addition to, compost, to bolster nutrients and improve the soil structure. You can also amend by adding fertilizers directly to correct specific imbalances in the soil. Natural fertilizers are best for this purpose. For more on those, see page 100.

Animal manure. Composted manure is much better as a soil amendment than a quick-release lawn fertilizer which can burn the grass. Most manures are rich sources of slow-release nitrogen that will provide a steady supply of the nutrient for a long time to come. When dug into topsoil, the manure also greatly improves the structure of the soil. Many raw manures, however, contain seeds from the plants eaten by the animal, which may include weeds. That's why the best form of manure for lawn soil amendment is composted manure. The heat of composting kills weed seeds. You can purchase bulk manure from the same sources as you would compost, but you can also get it free if you live within reasonable range of a farm with livestock, commercial stables, or a ranch. Most farm or ranch owners are more than happy to give the manure away if you're willing to clean it up. Whatever the source of the manure you use, it's always best to age it for at least six months to reduce the level of ammonia, a highly mobile source of nitrogen which can wash away, off gas, burn the lawn, or cause unhealthy levels of growth.

Green manure. This is a relatively new addition to the soil amendment line-up. The term refers to crops that are grown specifically to be dug back into the soil as enrichment. Depending on the crop, green manure can add a spectrum of nutrients to the soil. The process is bit lengthy because you have to grow a "cover crop" of one of a group of plants that serve the purpose. These include alfalfa, clover, soybeans, buckwheat and oats, among others. Some can be regularly mowed during the year they are growing, to maintain a neat and tidy appearance. Certain of these plants "fix" nitrogen (a method of storing it) in their roots. When they are plowed under, the green manure can serve the complete nitrogen needs for a lawn for up to a year.

Peat moss. Sphagnum peat moss is a widely used soil amendment that doesn't add much in the way of nutrients, but brings a big bang for the buck in terms of soil texture. Harvested from bogs around the world (most of the peat moss sold in the US comes from Canada), peat is a remarkable water sponge—holding up to 20 times its weight in moisture—which it then slowly releases. For this reason, peat is used most often to improve sandy soils. As a lawn amendment, you should add about 1 inch of peat for every 6 to 7 inches of topsoil. Be sure you know the pH of your soil, though, because peat moss may affect the acidity, lowering the pH.

Manure is a nitrogen-rich amendment that can greatly improve the water- and nutrient-retention properties of a lawn's soil. You can purchase composted cow or steer manure in bag form or by the yard.

Peat moss reduces the compaction potential of clay soils and improves water retention of sand soils.

Maintaining Proper Soil pH

In most lawns, the soil pH is fine. But when it's not, the variance can spell disaster for your new lawn. Imbalances in soil pH levels can be the result of heavy rainfall, the local geography, and other conditions. If your soil test shows a pH of less than 6.5 or higher than 7.5, it's wise to correct it before your new lawn goes in.

Fixing a pH imbalance should be done very carefully because it's easy to overdo and imbalance the soil to the opposite end of the scale. Ideally, if the imbalance is modest, use sulfur or lime in moderation to slowly make the change over a couple of seasons. For the same reason, measure these materials very carefully and be sure you know the correct treatment amounts. To correct acidity by raising pH, use lime. To fix high alkalinity and lower pH, use sulfur. Consult your local nursery professional or cooperative extension office agent for specific recommendations for your area, or you can use the general guidelines below regarding application amounts.

Lime. Ground limestone is a fine powder that is safe to work with because it is non-caustic. However, this type is very slow acting, taking weeks to fully alter the soil's pH. If you need faster results, you can use hydrated lime, known as quicklime. It's dangerous to work with, so exercise extreme caution. Pelleted lime is a safer version that combines quicklime and ground limestone in small pellets. The amount you use should be strictly controlled. Generally, to raise pH half a point (such as from 5.0 to 5.5), you should use 15–20 pounds per 1,000 square feet of lawn soil, or 30–35 if the soil is extra rich in loam. Generally, its wise to err on the side of caution, because you can always add more lime, even after you plant the new lawn.

Sulfur. Sulfur comes in two forms: powdered and granulated. Always use granulated if it's available because it's much easier to handle. However, with either form, use a facemask, gloves, and safety glasses. To lower pH a half point with sulfur, use about 3 pounds per 1,000 square feet of normal or slightly sandy soil. You may need up to 12 pounds per 1,000 square feet for extremely clay-heavy soils.

Test the soil about a month after you've laid the new lawn to measure if the amendment moved the pH into the recommended range. Apply a second treatment on top of the lawn as necessary.

Warning ▶

The fast-acting form of lime is called quicklime and it's caustic. Handling it can cause burns, and requires gloves, a respirator, safety glasses, and appropriate clothing. Quicklime should never be applied on a windy day and should not be brought into contact with skin. A safer way to handle this material is in pelleted form.

Thinking Green: Wood Ash ▶

If you use a wood-burning stove, you're creating an excellent amendment for treating acidic soil. Wood ash raises pH fairly quickly in the soil, and it brings with it a healthy dose of potassium and calcium—both nutrients essential to lawn health. Apply three times the amount of wood ash as you would lime, for the same square footage. Don't use ash from treated wood or wood that has been painted.

You can also use bone meal, crushed marble, or crushed oyster shells to treat acidic soil. And use sawdust, cottonseed meal, and peat moss to lower the soil pH. Consult with your local nursery or garden center expert about the correct amounts to use for your particular conditions.

APPLICATION GUIDELINES:

The following application rates are recommended for lawns:

pH Level	Rate (lbs/5,000 sq.ft.)
6.0 and above	30 lbs./1 Bag
5.5 to 6.0	60 lbs./2 Bags
5.0 to 5.5	90 lbs./3 Bags
Less than 5.0	120 lbs./4 Bags

Tips: For Established Trees &Shrubs, apply 5 lbs/1,000 sq. ft.
A soil test is helpful to determine the actual pH level.

SPREADER SETTINGS:

Spreader Type	Model	ENCAP FAST ACTING™ LIME Plus AST™ 30 lbs/5,000 sq.ft.
DROP	AGWAY DS 4500	4
DROP	SCOTTS ACCUGREEN 3000	4.5
BROADCAST	AGWAY SB 4000	7
BROADCAST	AGWAY TBS 4300	6
BROADCAST	AGWAY SB 6000 AG	7
BROADCAST	AGWAY TBS 4500 PAG	7
BROADCAST	AGWAY TBS 7000	3
BROADCAST	AGWAY TBS 6000 AG	6
BROADCAST	AGWAY SB 4500	8
BROADCAST	EARTHWAY 2030 PI	15
BROADCAST	EARTHWAY 2050	15
BROADCAST	LESCO COMMERCIAL PLUS	15
BROADCAST	SPYKER 76	6
BROADCAST	SPYKER 298	3
BROADCAST	SCOTTS SPEEDYGREEN 2000	7
BROADCAST	SCOTTS STANDARD	4
BROADCAST	SCOTTS DELUXE	4

Spreader settings are a guideline, actual applications may vary with age of equipment, gait of applicator and the smoothness of terrain.
Visit www.encap.net for more details.

*May not be applicable to all soil types. Please contact your local Cooperative Extension Service Office for recommendations regarding soil in your region.

In Wisconsin, there are no plant nutrient claims from the calcium in this product.
ENCAP® FAST ACTING™ LIME PLUS AST™

GUARANTEED ANALYSIS
Total Calcium (Ca)..38%
Calcium Carbonate (CaCO₃)..........................95.5%
Moisture (maximum).......................................1%
Neutralizing Value 94.6% Calcium Carbonate Equivalence (CCE)
Prilled from calcitic limestone   F1430
In Florida, this product requires 1902 pounds to be equal to one ton of standard liming material

Grading for Proper Drainage

The final step in preparing the bed for your new lawn is ensuring that the yard slopes correctly for proper drainage. That drainage is important for lawn health, but it's also essential to preventing water from draining into your house or undercutting and damaging your foundation.

Ideally, the lawn should slope away from the house (toward a street, road, or culvert), dropping 1 foot in height to every 50 feet of lawn. If the soil bed does not slope sufficiently, you should grade the surface before you install your lawn.

This basically entails moving dirt from a high point to a low point. It may mean more substantial digging down into the subsoil if you need to reverse a slope that runs toward your house. In this case, remove and store the valuable topsoil and dig out the subsoil, replacing the topsoil when you've established the proper grade.

Obviously, that could involve quite a bit of work. A large grading project calls for heavy equipment such as a front loader, and you'll probably want to hire professionals in that case. Make sure whoever you hire has experience in grading a residential yard, and that they are clear on how you want your topsoil handled.

No matter who is doing the grading work, it's a good time to add features such as an in-ground sprinkler system (see page 148), or wiring for low-voltage lights that are meant to line a sidewalk. It will be much easier to do any in-ground work before the lawn is planted.

All the usual caveats about checking with the local utilities, cable companies, and building departments before you dig apply when grading your property. But you also need to know where your septic system runs if you have one, and where your well-water supply line is, if you get your water from a well. When you're sure you are not going to create other problems while grading, it's time to get your tools together and complete the last step before planting your lawn.

Tools & Materials ▸

Pointed shovel	String line
Landscape rake	String level
Wheelbarrow	Stakes
Measuring tape	

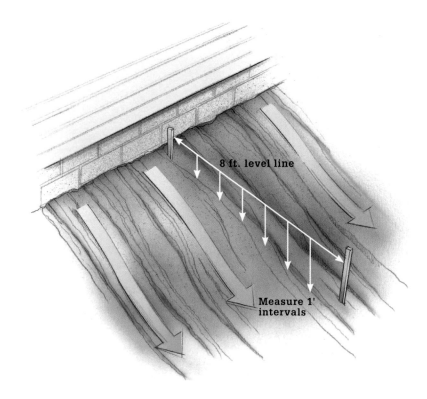

8 ft. level line

Measure 1' intervals

The soil bed for your lawn should slope away from your house and toward natural drainage points, such as streets with sewers. A slope of one foot per 50 feet of run is ideal: water runoff will not puddle, but it also won't drain so quickly to cause erosion.

How to Grade a Lawn

Drive a stake into the soil at the base of the foundation and another at least 8 ft. out into the yard along a straight line from the first stake. Attach a string fitted with a line level to the stakes and level it. Measure and flag the string with tape at 1-ft. intervals. Measure down from the string at the tape flags, recording your measurements to use as guidelines for adding or removing soil to create a correct grade.

Working away from the base of the house, add soil to low areas until they reach the desired height. Using a garden rake, evenly distribute the soil over a small area. Measure down from the 1-ft. markings as you work to make sure that you are creating a ¾" per 1 ft. pitch. Add and remove soil as needed until soil is evenly sloped, then move on to the next area and repeat the process.

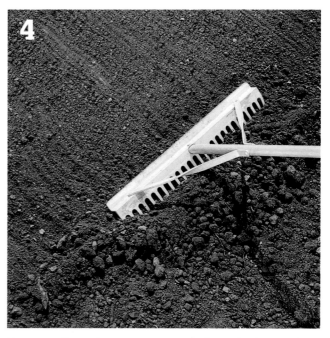

Use a hand tamp or a roller to lightly compact the soil. Don't overtamp the soil or it could become too dense to grow a healthy lawn or plants. Add a little more soil after tamping as a seed bed for the grass seed or sod.

Use a grading rake to remove any rocks or clumps. Starting at the foundation, pull the rake in a straight line down the slope. Dispose of any rocks or construction debris. Repeat the process, working on one section at a time until the entire area around the house is graded.

Laying Sod

Ensuring the success of a lawn created from sod begins before the delivery of the sod. Sod doesn't age well, so you want to install it as quickly as possible. Have all your tools and equipment prepared, have any helpers you're going to need on hand, and be ready to get to work as soon as the sod arrives.

When it is delivered, check to see you've received all the sod you ordered. Have the sod stacked in a shady area. Inspect the sod closely. Fresh sod will be moist and cool to the touch. If the sod is hot, it means the process of decomposing has begun. You should also check for uneven top growth, yellowing blades, and curling edges—all unwelcome signs that the sod has been sitting around for too long.

Once you're satisfied that the sod is in good condition, spray it down well using a hose equipped with a nozzle attachment set to mist. When you start work, it's a good idea to moisten both the roll of sod you're preparing to lay, and the strip of soil the sod's going on top of.

Although sod is essentially an instant lawn to the eye, newly laid sod is still vulnerable. In addition to the post-installation watering you'll have to do until the grass is fully established and actively growing, you'll want to keep all traffic off the lawn for several weeks if possible. It's especially important to keep pets off the lawn, because animal urine is fairly toxic to new sod. With some basic protection and follow-up care, your sodded lawn will, in month's time, look like it's always been there. *Note: Soil should be properly graded, amended, and raked out prior to laying sod.*

Tools & Materials ▸

Large sharp knife	Sod
Wheelbarrow	Plywood scrap (for
Drum roller	kneeling platform)
Trowel	Wood stakes
Straightedge	String line

Laying sod is the quickest and most satisfying (and also the most expensive) way to create an instant lawn.

How to Lay Sod

Check all the sod as soon as it's delivered. Look for damage, disease, or signs of insect infestation. Feel to make sure the sod is not hot, indicating that it has begun decomposing. Store the sod in a cool, shaded area, keeping it moist until you lay it.

Lay the first strip of sod along a straight edge such as a front sidewalk. Butt it to the edge as tightly as possible without overlapping the surface. Mist the soil lightly before setting the sod.

Alternative: If there is no straight edge to use as a guide, such as along a property line with no sidewalk, create one with stakes and string.

Continue the row of sod by butting the next strip up tight against the end of the first. Be sure there is no gap, and that the strips do not overlap.

(continued)

Cut the first strip in the second row as necessary to create a staggered "brick" pattern. Use a large, sharp knife, or sharpened trowel.

Fill any low areas as you lay the strips, to ensure there are no voids underneath the sod. Trowel in topsoil or compost to level each individual area.

As you work, stop about every 20 to 30 minutes and spray the strips you've laid—as well as the stack of sod—with enough water to keep them moist.

If you need to butt strips at an angle to one another, overlap them, and cut completely through both strips with your knife or sharpened trowel.

8

At curves in sidewalks or paths, lay the end of the last strip over the path, and cut the sod along the edging of the path surface. Cut the sod snug, because you can cut again if you need to, but you shouldn't add thin scraps of sod as filler.

9

If the final row of sod will need to be cut to width, lay a full-size row on the outer edge, and cut the next-to-last row to fit. Use a straightedge, such as a large metal carpenter's square, long metal ruler, or level.

10

Roll the lawn with a roller at least half-full with water to ensure there are no air pockets and that the sod is firmly in contact with the soil.

Planting Sod on a Slope ▸

One of the advantages of installing sod instead of spreading seed is that it is far better for growing lawns on a slope. But sod strips can still slide out of position. Secure sod strips on a slope by pegging them with metal pegs or with home-made tapered wooden stakes.

(continued)

Check the strips for separation gaps or any areas that you have cut short. Fill these with a combination of sterile soil and grass seed that matches the species in the sod.

Water the lawn every day—unless it rains—until you are sure the grass is established and growing (usually a little more than a week).

Prepping Soil for Sod ▸

Amending the topsoil and raking the surface out flat is often all the prep work you'll need to do prior to laying sod. But you can take steps to help the sod root securely. The quicker and more completely it roots, the faster and more robust your new lawn will grow in.

Use a leaf rake to scratch shallow furrows in the soil (as seen in the photo at right) in the direction you'll be laying the soil. Similar to the way raised tire treads help a tire grip the road, these furrows will help the sod bond down to the soil.

You can also give your sod a head start by spreading a starter fertilizer over the top of the soil before laying the sod. This will guarantee that the new sod has all the nutrients it needs to begin growing strong. Apply starter fertilizer strictly according the instructions on the bag or box—more is not usually better in the case of sod. And don't ever be tempted to spread a general synthetic fertilizer because you may prompt a flush of top growth at the expense of strong roots—leading to big problems down the road.

How to Plant a New Lawn from Plugs

Use stakes and string to create guides 8" to 12" apart over the length of the lawn surface. Make the holes for the plugs with a bulb-planting tool, staggering them to create a checkerboard pattern.

Plant the first row of plugs along the first guideline, so that the plugs are spaced the same distance apart as you spaced the rows.

Remove the string and stakes and water the plugs well, keeping them moist until they are obviously established.

Alternate: Plant sprigs (individual plants) just as you would plugs, but don't dig holes. Simply push them into the soil spaced a few inches apart. For even coverage you can set up string lines; but spacing them out by eye will work, too.

Planting a Lawn From Seed

Seeding is the traditional way (and certainly the least expensive method) to grow a new lawn. It is also one of the trickiest because so many things can go wrong, from seed that doesn't germinate to a run-in with a flock of hungry swallows. If you choose this method for growing a new lawn, give your lawn the best chance possible by being exacting in each step of the seeding process.

Everything starts with the seed. By shopping carefully for your seed, you take the first steps toward maximizing the seed's potential. The next trick is to make sure the seed is set down in the right way and the right place. Drop spreaders are best for this. Because they drop the seed directly below the hopper, it's easier to tell where the seed is going, and to know exactly where to overlap the rows. It's common on larger lawns to use a broadcast or rotary spreader because the width of each row will be three times or the more the size of drop spreader rows. If you use a broadcast spreader, you'll need to be very diligent about where the seed is going to ensure an even starting growth for your lawn.

Once you've distributed all the seed and laid down a protective layer over it, you've still got work to do. One of the keys to helping as many seeds as possible germinate is to make sure that the seeds never completely dry out. This means you have to water the seeded area lightly, several times a day. You can cut back on the watering to a couple times a day once your seedlings sprout, but you still need to give a lot more moisture than an established lawn will need. After three or four weeks, you may also need to overseed areas not filling in because the seeds were in shade, or they were not spread evenly.

Tools & Materials ▸

Drop spreader
Leaf rake
Drum roller

Grass seed
Grass fabric
  or mulch

A drop spreader is often used for fertilizing, but can also be used to apply seed. It ensures even grass seed coverage for a more uniform lawn. But it is essential to regularly clean and maintain your spreader. A poorly functioning unit translates to improper feeding and possible damage to the lawn.

How to Seed a New Lawn

With the soil prepared as described on page 72, spread the seed. Set the drop spreader to the setting listed on the seed bag, test the dispersal rate on a driveway or sidewalk, and begin seeding.

Rake the seed into the surface of the soil. Drag a leaf rake upside down over the surface to rake in the seeds. Rake gently to prevent dispersing the seeds too much.

Proper Seed Dispersal ▶

Regardless of whether you're using a drop, broadcast, or even a hand-held spreader, the goal is to have a nice, even dispersal across the entire area of the soil. Check to ensure you are dropping the right number of seeds per square inch, as recommended by the seed company and listed on the seed bag. Use a square to count seeds and check the dispersal in different areas of the lawn as you spread the seed, and make adjustments as necessary.

(continued)

3

Water drum empty

Roll the surface of the lawn with an empty drum roller. The goal is to press the seeds firmly into the soil without crushing them.

4

Water the surface immediately. Protect the newly seeded lawn with ropes or tape to keep dogs and cats off the surface. Cover the lawn with clean straw or degradable garden fabric to help ensure germination and retain moisture. Spun bonded poly mesh will also protect the seeds against birds, but it is not readily degradable.

Spreading by Hand ▸

Drop or broadcast spreaders are effective on lawns of any size, but for much smaller lawns, such as a modest patch behind a townhouse, it is easier and quicker to spread seed by hand. You can use a handheld crank spreader, or even just broadcast handfuls of seed as you walk along. Either way, check to be sure that the seed is broadcast evenly across the soil in the concentration recommended on the seed bag. And remember, too much seed can be as bad as too little.

If you opt to spread seed with a handheld spreader, walk at a constant rate and hold the spreader as steady and level as possible to achieve the correct distribution of seed.

Hydroseeding ▶

Hydroseeding is a relatively new alternative to growing a lawn from seed or sod. It's quick, easy, and has a great success rate. The process involves spraying a mix of grass seed, water, and fertilizer that has been combined with a base of fiber or recycled paper. Other elements such as soil inoculants are sometimes added, but the main idea is that the dense liquid mix gets pumped through a sprayer, and is sprayed across the prepared soil surface. The wet fiber or paper base sticks to the soil, holding the seed in place, while keeping it moist and protected from the elements and birds.

In time, the seeds germinate and sprout, and the fiber or paper base decomposes, adding to the soil's structure and slowly releasing fertilizer.

It's a highly effective process, is one that can be done in a fraction of the time it would take to sod a large lawn, and is even quicker than seeding. Hydroseeding is also an excellent option for troublespots such as slopes. Because the seeds are contained in such a beneficial medium, the germination rate for hydroseeding exceeds that of seeded lawns, and the grass usually sprouts faster. In most cases, you'll quite possibly be mowing the lawn in less than a month.

Expense wise, this option usually falls somewhere between the cost of sod and the cost of seed. But it's not a DIY project; getting the blend right and spraying correctly so that the coverage is spot on takes a professional. The one major downside is that many hydroseeding contractors offer a very limited selection of grass seed varieties. Hydroseeding should be done at the beginning of the growing season for your type of grass.

Maintaining Your Lawn

Maintaining a weed-, disease-, and problem-free lawn isn't rocket science; it just requires correct maintenance practices, done at the right time on regular intervals.

The first step is to make sure you have all the tools necessary to properly take care of your lawn. Those tools should be in good repair, which makes any lawn care job easier.

Mowing is the most regular of lawn-maintenance chores. But there are distinctively right and wrong ways of mowing the lawn. The wrong way doesn't just make your lawn look bad, it opens it up to infection from diseases and attack by pests. So it pays to make sure your lawnmower is in good running condition and that you mow at the best time and in the best way for your lawn.

Ensuring the grass gets all the water it needs is another good lawn-maintenance practice. And lawn maintenance also involves several less regular, but no less important, tasks. Fertilizing, aerating, and shutting your lawn down properly for the winter (or whenever it goes dormant), all impact how well your lawn grows and looks.

In this chapter:
- Feeding Your Lawn
- Mowing Fundamentals
- Mowing the Lawn
- Trimming & Edging
- Water & Your Lawn
- Winterizing the Lawn

Lawn-Care Hand Tools

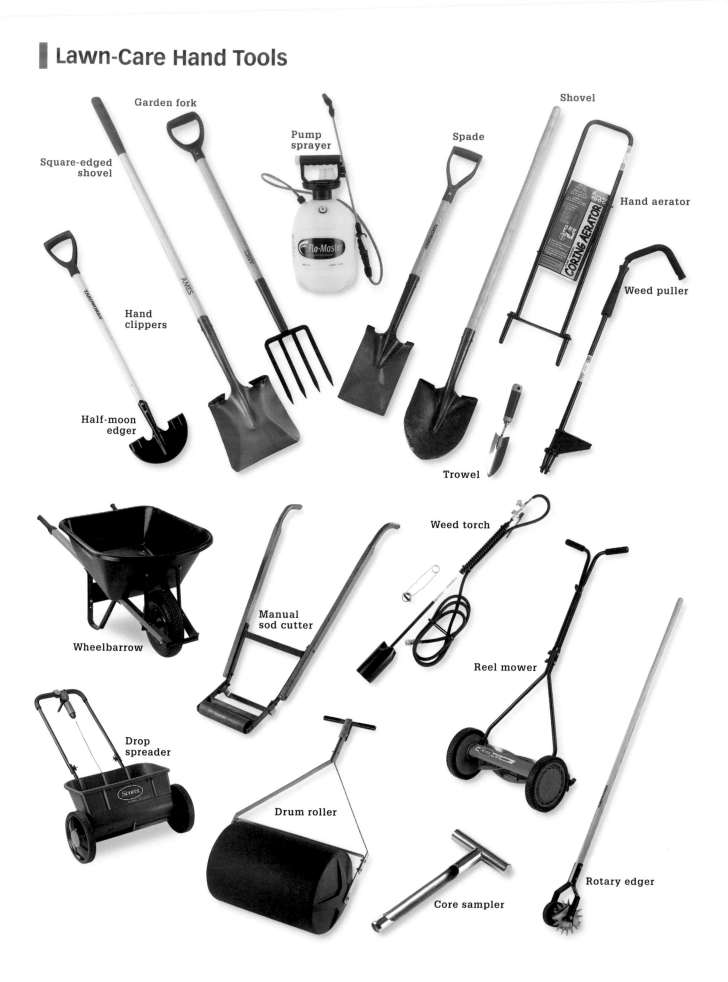

Garden fork

Square-edged shovel

Pump sprayer

Spade

Shovel

Hand aerator

Hand clippers

Weed puller

Half-moon edger

Trowel

Wheelbarrow

Manual sod cutter

Weed torch

Reel mower

Drop spreader

Drum roller

Core sampler

Rotary edger

Lawn-Care Power Tools

Power edger

Power cultivator

Push mower

Garden sprayer

String trimmer

Power shears

Power blower/vacuum

Rental Power Equipment

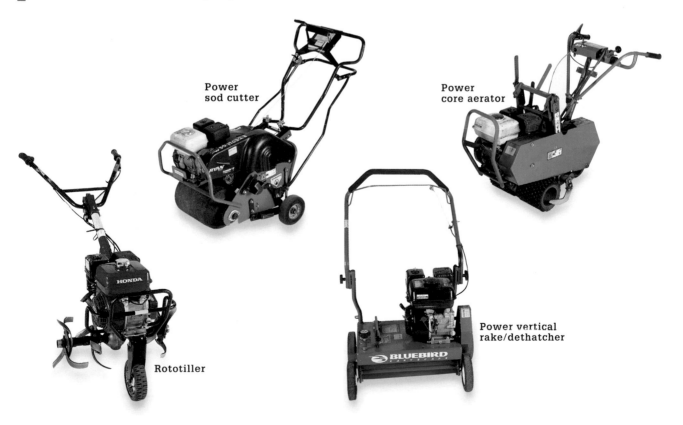

Power sod cutter

Power core aerator

Rototiller

Power vertical rake/dethatcher

Feeding Your Lawn

A lawn can exist with very little help from the soil, but if you want an enviable patch of green you really need to stock the pantry for your grass. The term "feeding the lawn" is actually a bit of a misnomer; when you fertilize you're just giving the soil nutrients that the individual grass plants need to perform photosynthesis. As most of us learned in elementary school, that's the process through which individual leaves of grass use the sun's energy to convert water and carbon dioxide into sugars the plant uses to grow. In other words, it feeds itself. Just the same, it's as if you were feeding the lawn because the grass needs the nutrients the soil contains to survive.

The trick is giving the grass just the right amount and right balance of nutrients at just the right time to help it grow as consistently perfect as possible. You won't need a degree in chemistry to master the fine art of fertilizing a lawn, but you do need a basic understanding of the nutrients the grass needs and how it uses them.

You learned a little bit about the three macronutrients in Testing Your Soil on page 30. But if nitrogen, phosphorous, and potassium are the big three, they certainly aren't the only components of fertilizer. Nor are they the only vitamins the lawn

hungers for. They are just the nutrients it uses in the largest amounts.

Any lawn also relies on a steady supply of smaller amounts of secondary nutrients and various micronutrients. Each plays a lesser or greater role in lawn health. But the best protection for any lawn is the right balance of nutrients—almost as important as the amounts of each.

The form the fertilizer takes will affect how readily available it is to the grass roots, as well as how long it persists in the soil. The two basic forms are liquid and dry. Both can supply the nutrients your grass needs but liquid fertilizer is generally more quick-acting and easier to prepare. It doesn't last as long as granular types do. It also takes a bit of skill to apply liquid fertilizer evenly. That's one of the reasons the majority of homeowners use dry fertilizer for regular lawn feedings.

As you proceed through this section, it's a good idea to have your lawn soil tests on hand, and give them some thought as you read about the different nutrients. When you're done, you should have a pretty exact idea of just how much of each nutrient you want to feed the lawn, and what form you want those nutrients to take.

Granular fertilizer is easy to spread evenly with a spreader, so many homeowners choose it over liquid fertilizer.

Variable Appetites ▸

Grass type affects fertilizer consumption. For instance, Bermuda grass and Kentucky bluegrass are pretty much hogs when consuming nutrients, while centipede grass and Bahia are light eaters. Like many other particulars about lawn care, there is debate about appropriate nutrient amounts for any given turfgrass, so it's a good idea to speak with your nursery professional or local cooperative extension office expert about the nutrient needs of your particular grass species and variety. Also talk with neighbors who seem to be having success with their lawns. The following numbers are a good baseline for the most common types of turfgrass. The amounts listed represent the pounds of nitrogen each grass will need on average in a year to support a healthy, typical, 2,000-square-foot lawn.

Cool Season:	
Kentucky bluegrass	±10
Ryegrass	±5
Tall fescue	±6
Perennial Ryegrass	±5

Warm Season:	
Bermuda	±8
St. Augustine	±8
Zoysia	±6
Centipede grass	±4

Transition Grasses:	
Buffalograss	±3
Blue Grama	±3

Mixing a liquid fertilizer is easy and quick, but sprayed fertilizer is available to the grass for only a brief period.

Successfully fertilizing with dry fertilizer means exacting measurements and a thorough watering to ensure the nutrients reach the grass roots.

Nitrogen, Phosphorous & Potassium

Of the three major nutrients, nitrogen has the biggest direct impact on the lawn, specifically in regards to visible growth and color. Nitrogen is crucial to chlorophyll, the metabolic component that makes grass green. Your lawn consumes more nitrogen than it does any single other nutrient. As far as fertilizers (natural or synthetic) go, pay the most attention to the nitrogen content.

Nitrogen is actually all around us, as an inert gas in the air (actually, almost 80 percent of the air). You'd think that grass could get all it needs from the air, but that's unfortunately not the way it works. That gas needs to be converted for use in plants, including grass. It's why organic farmers plant special nitrogen-grabbing "cover" crops that are plowed under at the end of the growing season (clover does the same thing in your lawn, but most consider it a weed and a blemish on their carefully cultivated green carpet). These plants convert airborne nitrogen, making it available in the soil in a process called nitrogen fixing.

Turfgrass, unlike cover crops, is a heavy net consumer of nitrogen and thus, needs a reliable consistent supply of the nutrient. When your grass experiences nitrogen deficiency it turns pale and yellow and may even start thinning out. But most lawns don't get that bad unless they are stressed in some other way as well. When grass plants have a steady supply of the right amount of nitrogen, shoots and stems grow thick and strong. That helps prevent weeds, disease, and pests from making a home among the grass.

Both synthetic and natural fertilizers can supply nitrogen. The debate over which is better is a hotly contested one, but the key difference in feeding a lawn is that most natural versions supply only slow-release nitrogen, while synthetic types offer either fast-release or slow-release nitrogen in their formulations.

THE TWO PS

Phosphorous (represented as "P" on a fertilizer bag's label) and potassium (represented as "K") live in the shadow of nitrogen when it comes to fertilizing your lawn, but that doesn't mean they aren't significant. In fact, severe deficiencies of either can compromise lawn health. But in most cases, these nutrients stay in the soil so long that deficiencies are rare, and additional amounts delivered via fertilizer are usually very modest.

Phosphorous is most important for new root growth, making it a key nutrient for seedlings. It's wise, for instance, to boost the amount of phosphorous in the fertilizer you use on a warm-season grass, before you overseed for winter growth with a cool-season grass seed. A phosphorous-heavy mix is a good idea as the first feeding after planting a lawn from seed as well. Phosphorous is slow-acting and most of its benefits are only apparent below the soil. It will spur new root growth over weeks and the result will be a healthy top growth over time.

Potassium is the backup player of the big three. That's because it helps grass plants endure times of stress, keeping cool-season grasses alive over tough winters, and helping any grass ride out fluxuating moisture levels. Potassium is, like phosphorous, slow and steady. The best time to use a high-potassium fertilizer is in the fall, to help the lawn survive the tough months to come.

Very bright green color is a sign that a lawn is saturated with nitrogen. Too much nitrogen can spur what appears to be lush, green top growth at the expense of root development.

Secondary Lawn Nutrients

The three secondary nutrients essential to soil health and lawn growth are calcium, magnesium, and sulfur. Deficiencies in these signal a very unhealthy soil or at least a pH imbalance. Calcium and magnesium are ingredients in the lime that is used raise the soil's pH, while sulfur is used to lower it.

Calcium helps stabilize pH and loosens soil, serving as a mild conditioning agent. More importantly, this mineral strengthens plant cell walls, contributing to strong root and top growth. A complete lack of calcium translates to development of weak roots and stunted shoots.

Magnesium also helps condition soil, acting as a bonding agent to maintain a strong soil structure. It's also an important element in chlorophyll, and in that way, contributes to food production within a grass plant.

Sulfur is primarily used in relation to soil pH. But it's also a necessary ingredient in key amino acids and proteins used in grass plant functions.

MICRONUTRIENTS

Rounding out the elements that contribute to lawn and soil health are a group of nutrients present in much smaller amounts than macronutrients. There are seven of these and each has its own role. Boron promotes the development of flowers, which in grass assists overall growth (the grass plant is always trying to get to the flowering stage and forever being stymied by the lawnmower). Chlorine helps stabilize soil structure, while copper promotes plant growth by serving as a component of chlorophyll. Iron is perhaps the most important micronutrient, and is an essential catalyst to chlorophyll creation. As such, iron is one of the few micronutrients that can make its absence known; given a lack of iron, the grass leaves will turn yellow. Manganese is crucial for the function of photosynthesis and aids grass plants in processing nitrogen. Molybdenum promotes nitrogen fixing, while zinc helps the formation of starch for the plants to use in processing energy.

Although yellowing of the grass can be a sign of nitrogen deficiency, if you've fed the lawn nitrogen and it's still yellow, chances are that the soil is low in iron.

Synthetic Fertilizers

The actual act of fertilizing a lawn is not all that complex. But figuring out exactly what type of fertilizer you should use, and how much, is a far different matter. Not only does the type of grass and where you live affect the amount of fertilizer your lawn will need, it also influences timing. And to make matters a little more confusing, just how often a lawn should be fed is a matter of no small debate—even among professionals.

How often and how much you feed your lawn depends first on whether you choose to use a synthetic, mass-produced fertilizer, or whether you've opted to go all natural or organic. If you're like the vast majority of homeowners throughout the country, you most likely use synthetic fertilizer.

That choice is usually driven by how easy synthetic fertilizers are to use. Synthetics offer the choice of fast- or slow-acting nitrogen, where the nitrogen in natural fertilizers is usually slow-release. Synthetic formulations also deliver greater amounts of nutrients in one shot than natural types do. This means you'll use less of them, which translates to less expense.

Of course organic lawn-care proponents would say these advantages are more than offset by the downsides to using synthetic fertilizers: a strong potential for overuse and damage to the lawn from excess nitrogen; and misuse that results in damage to the environment as excess fertilizer makes its way into the water system both locally and regionally.

If you use synthetics, you can address these concerns by being very careful in what type of fertilizer you use, how much, and how and when you apply it. Careful fertilizing practices ensure that most if not all of the fertilizer remains in the soil until it is used by the grass. Signs of overfertilization are pretty clear. They include succulent grass blades almost full to bursting with moisture, blades that when squeezed or rubbed leave your fingers green, and deep green growth so dense and top heavy that individual grass blades flop over.

Buying the right synthetic fertilizer mix starts with measuring the square footage of your lawn. Bagged fertilizer is usually calculated for a 1,000-square-foot yard. You'll need to factor your square footage to determine how many bags (or fractions of bags) you'll need to use.

In addition to normal formulations, you can buy timed-release fertilizers in which the particles are coated to slowly release nutrients over a much longer period than regular fertilizer. These types of fertilizers are more expensive, but they last much longer and may even prevent the need for additional feedings. On the downside, though, timed-release fertilizers are not controllable—the nutrients, and especially nitrogen, may be feeding the lawn during periods when it should not be fed.

You'll also find so-called combination fertilizers that include herbicides or pesticides added to the fertilizer mix. Although these can be quite handy as all-in-one solutions, you don't have the control

Slow Release vs. Quick Release ▸

There are basically two types of nitrogen in fertilizers: slow release and quick release. Slow-release versions feed the grass plants a more moderate dose over time and are less likely to burn the grass. You'll also need fewer applications because the fertilizer lasts longer.

Quick-release types are great for fast "green-ups" and, unlike their slower counterparts, they make the nitrogen available in colder weather. The cost is less as well. But quick-release nitrogen is more likely to leach from the soil in the presence of heavy drainage, meaning it can make its way into sewers, waterways, water tables, and other areas where it can have a

negative environmental impact. It is also more likely to kill beneficial microorganisms, damaging the health of the soil.

Some types of synthetic fertilizers combine both fast- and slow-release particles. Most organic fertilizers are just slow-release by their very nature, feeding the lawn a modest, continuous, and balanced stream of nutrients. Fast-release fertilizers include ammonium nitrate, ammonium sulfate, calcium nitrate, and urea, among others. Slow-release types include activated sludge, sulfur-coated urea, soybean meal, bone meal, composted manure, and methylene urea.

over application that you would by applying the components separately. Combination fertilizers are best used as a pre-treatment for common and widespread weeds such as crabgrass.

Whatever type or brand of fertilizer you buy, keep in mind that you are purchasing a powerful chemical mix. It's extremely important—for your lawn and garden, your family's health, and the well-being of the environment—that you follow the manufacturer's directions to the letter and exercise diligence and caution whenever you fertilize the lawn.

Decoding the Label ▶

The label on a bag of fertilizer contains a great deal of useful information, but you need to know how it applies to your lawn before you make your purchase. The biggest numbers are the most important, representing the relative amounts of nitrogen, phosphorous, and potassium in the mix (N-P-K). The numbers are the percentage of that component that makes up the bag's contents. For instance, a 10-10-10 formulation would indicate that 10 percent of the contents are nitrogen, 10 percent are phosphorous and 10 percent are potassium. The remaining 70 percent of the bag's contents is comprised of inert materials and ingredients that help deliver or hold the nutrients in a form that facilitates use by the lawn's root system.

You can use these numbers to figure out just how much nitrogen is being delivered per 1,000 square feet (the standard baseline measure used on most bags). To figure out how many pounds of nitrogen you're delivering to your 1,000 square foot lawn, using the example above, you would multiply the percentage of nitrogen (.10) by the overall weight of the bag (standard bags of fertilizer are 15.5 pounds). So, .10 × 15.5 = 1.55 pounds of nitrogen. Divide that number by the number of 1,000 square-foot segments of coverage listed on the label (let's say 2,000) and you discover that it will deliver .78 pounds of nitrogen (1.55/2) per 1,000 square feet.

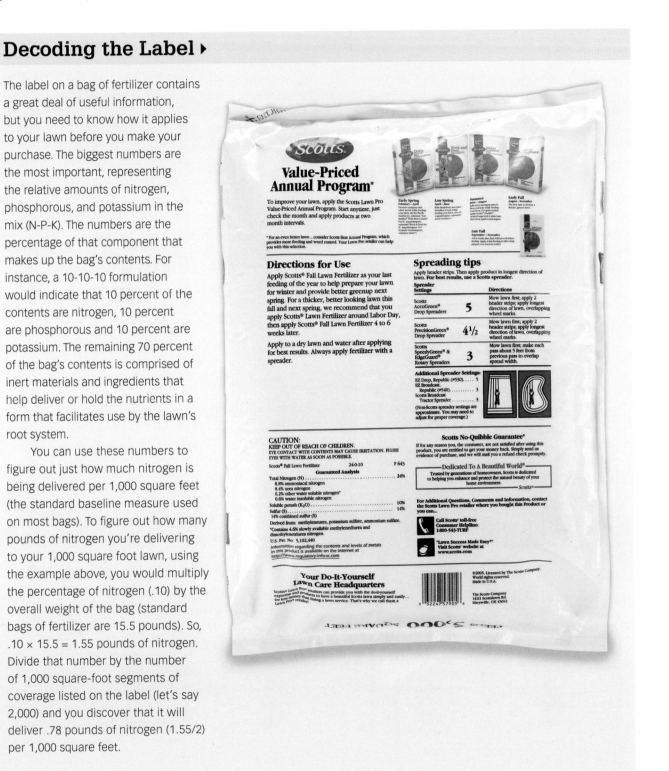

Natural Fertilizers

To understand natural fertilizers it helps to understand what natural means in terms of fertilizers. Natural is often confused with organic, but the two can actually be quite different. Natural pertains to any product from a plant or animal. Organic, in its truest form, precludes any chemicals. So while you can consider a plant-based fertilizer natural, it's not considered organic by purists if the soil or the plant was treated with any artificial chemicals such as pesticides.

That said, there are a range of effective and environmentally friendly natural fertilizers. They break down into two basic categories: animal products and plant products.

Animal-based products such as cow manure and bat guano can make rich fertilizers, but working with the materials can be a distinctly unpleasant experience. And, more recently, concern about animal-borne diseases has given some homeowners pause about using these types of fertilizer on their lawns. Still, animal-based fertilizers are incredibly rich sources of nutrients for your grass.

Manures are rich in nitrogen and other nutrients, are plentiful, and fairly inexpensive. Manure is usually composted before being used as a fertilizer. The downside to these types of fertilizers—and many other natural types—is that they release nitrogen slowly and unpredictably. The soil needs to be warm enough so that the microorganisms that break the fertilizer down and release the nitrogen are active.

Fish emulsion is just another way of saying fish manure. This is a nutrient-packed fertilizer containing as much as 10 percent nitrogen. Pure fish emulsion can be a little on the pricey side, but it stands out among natural fertilizers because unlike the slow-acting nature of most of these, fish emulsion acts quickly and can even be used to green-up the lawn.

Feather meal

Alfalfa meal

Bat guano is even more expensive, but is incredibly rich in key nutrients.

Meals are ground animal parts that can be rich sources of nitrogen. Blood meal, for instance, is 12 to 15 percent nitrogen, while feather meal is almost as rich. Bonemeal is, meanwhile, a mother lode of phosphorous and calcium. The downside is that meals are all expensive, and should not be used directly as fertilizers because they can do as much damage to top growth as the benefits they bring to the soil. They are, however, often used in natural fertilizer blends.

Plant-based products are increasing in popularity and many, such as seaweed, have been used throughout history as rich sources of nutrients, as well as amendments to improve soil structure.

Alfalfa meal is a key ingredient in many blended natural fertilizers. Containing around 3 percent nitrogen, it can be used in its raw form as a soil amendment.

Soybean meal is another common addition to natural fertilizer blends because of its very high nitrogen content and its wide availability. Like alfalfa meal, you'll find soybean meal at farm supply outlets, if you want to use it as a soil amendment.

Seaweed is a time-tested soil additive, which is why it too is included in many bagged natural fertilizers. Although it contains a modest amount of nitrogen (about 1 percent) it contains many organic compounds that aid grass plants in vigorous growth and seed and seedling development.

The easiest way to realize the benefits of natural fertilizers is to buy a bagged blend. Like their synthetic counterparts, these bags list the N-P-K amounts right on the front, so you can use them just as you would a synthetic version.

Natural fertilizer

Thinking Green: Soil Inoculants ▸

Soil inoculant is a relatively new lawn treatment that is being embraced by homeowners looking to go natural in their lawn maintenance. Inoculants aren't fertilizers or pesticides, but are usually applied in a similar fashion. As their name implies they inoculate the soil against pests and diseases. Along the way, some types assist in the uptake of nutrients by grass roots, and can increase grass plants' strength and vitality.

Mycorrhizae is one of the most commonly used lawn inoculants. These are beneficial fungi that attach to the roots of grass plants and help them take in water and nutrients. Added to natural fertilizers mycorrhizae can increase grass plant vitality, increase growth and green-up rates, and help prevent the onset of diseases.

Rhizobia have long been a part of the success of legumes such as clover. The bacteria works by infiltrating plant roots and setting up nodes that allow it to fix nitrogen from the air.

There are other inoculants, such as algae, that have similar beneficial affects on turfgrass. They can all be added to natural lawn fertilizers, but you should save your money if you fertilize using synthetics. Research has shown most natural inoculants are shut down in the presence of synthetic additives.

Applying Fertilizer

Once you've worked out the type of fertilizer you'll use and the N-P-K blend you'll need, it's time to apply that fertilizer to the lawn. The process is done with a spreader, and should be done carefully to prevent fertilizer from going where you don't intend it to go.

The best way to do that is by using a walk-behind drop spreader, the most popular kind. It is the most effective type because you maintain control over exactly where you lay the fertilizer. There is a much smaller chance that you will spread fertilizer onto any adjacent areas such as flowerbeds, where the fertilizer could cause damage.

However, if you have a large yard, you may prefer to use a broadcast spreader because it covers the area much more quickly than any other type.

Whatever the case, before you begin actually fertilizing, you should take your empty spreader out for a spin. Roll it over the grass and walk up and back a few times just to get the feel of keeping a steady walking rhythm. It may seem silly, but this could

Spreader
Push broom

Fertilizer
Gloves

easily prevent the odd-looking lawn that results from having fertilized some spots too much and others too little. Then you'll want to do the test outlined on page 104 to make doubly sure you've got your pacing down.

After you've finished, give the spreader a good rinse so that no fertilizer remains in the hopper, stuck to the frame, or on the wheels (you may be using a different blend next time you use the spreader and mixing blends is not a good idea). Wash the spreader on the lawn, and let it dry completely before you put it away.

Timing the Application ▸

When you fertilize is every bit as important as how, and there are actually two "whens," the time of day and the time during the year. It's always best to spread fertilizer in the morning, when the grass is still wet with dew (and the sun is not directly overhead). The moisture will keep the fertilizer down. But you should still water thoroughly afterward to ensure the fertilizer particles make it all the way down to the soil.

The time of the year that you should fertilize depends on whether your lawn is warm- or cool-season grass. Cool-season grasses should be fertilized in mid fall, a few weeks before the lawn goes dormant. Fertilize warm-season grasses in early spring, just as the weather warms and the grass prepares a flush of growth for early summer.

Of course, you may want to fertilize with smaller amounts at different times. Give a cool-season lawn a second feeding in late summer, just as the weather cools for fall. A third can be done in late spring. For warm-season lawns, add a second feeding in mid summer, and a third at the end of summer, right before the weather cools off.

Always load your drop spreader on a hard surface so you can sweep up spillage instead of letting it remain in the lawn.

Choosing Your Spreader

Deciding on a spreader is an important decision that can affect many of the lawn maintenance chores you'll do over time. The right spreader can make the job easier; the wrong one can damage the lawn by spreading materials unevenly over the surface.

HOSE-END APPLICATOR

This is a simple spreader used only for liquid fertilizers, herbicides, and pesticides. It's the easiest spreader to use, but also the least efficient. Simply mix the material into the screw-on container and attach the applicator nozzle to the end of your hose. The water under pressure mixes with the container's ingredients and disperses them with the water spray. Even coverage is difficult to achieve, and liquid fertilizer washes out of the soil very quickly.

HAND-HELD SPREADER

If you have a steady hand, a keen eye, and an attention to detail, a hand-held spreader can work well for you. This type of spreader is used for overseeding, topdressing, and feeding the lawn. It is, however, limited in coverage and actually somewhat more work during the actual task than a push spreader would be. Fill the hopper and walk along at a steady rate, turning the crank at a steady rate. Although you can achieve even coverage with a little practice and patience, dispersing just the right amount of fertilizer or seed is difficult. Consequently, hand-held spreaders are usually limited to small areas of lawn over which using a larger spreader would be impractical.

DROP SPREADER

The most common type of spreader, the drop spreader has a simple hopper with a plate that blocks holes in the bottom until it's opened with a lever on the handle of the spreader. When held open, the vents drop seed, fertilizer, or other material in an even stream 1½ to 2 feet wide. This makes it easy to see where you've laid the fertilizer so that you don't overlap strips too much. However, the modest width means that covering large lawns translates to quite a lot of walking.

BROADCAST (ROTARY) SPREADER

This type features a hopper with sides that taper to a round or oval bottom. Like a drop spreader, the broadcast spreader has holes in the bottom of the hopper that are opened and closed with a handle-mounted lever. As the material drops out of the hopper, it is distributed through a spinning horizontal disc that is turned by the action of the wheels, distributing seed or fertilizer in a much broader swath than a drop spreader would. Although this allows you to cover a much greater area in a shorter time, it also presents some difficulty in determining the outer edges of each pass you take. That means that overfertilizing areas between passes is a real possibility with a broadcast spreader, as is spreading fertilizer or grass seed onto garden beds or into shrubs.

Hand-held spreader

Drop spreader

Broadcast (rotary) spreader

Hose-end applicator

Checking Spreader Accuracy

You need to trust that the spreader you're using is spreading correctly according to the setting you have it on. Because you're operating on the manufacturer's recommendation for the amount of fertilizer to be applied, if the setting is incorrect, you can be applying much less—or even much more—than you intended. Either case is going to lead to some less-than-desirable results in lawn growth.

Calibrating a spreader is not the easiest procedure, and it involves a bit of math. Many homeowners who realize that their spreader is not delivering fertilizer or seed exactly as the setting indicates opt to buy a new unit, because spreaders are relatively inexpensive. However, if you want to dive in and save the money, half an hour or so is all it takes to fine-tune the spreader you have. Just make sure to clean up any fertilizer after you test for calibration.

Calibrating a Drop Spreader

Start by measuring the width of your spreader's hopper bottom. Standard widths are 1 foot, 1½ feet, and 2 feet Wire a large catch pan underneath the hopper to catch the fertilizer. Next, find a long solid surface such as a parking lot, and mark off an even distance such as 50 feet (the longer, the better). Fill the spreader with fertilizer and open the hopper as you walk at a steady pace along the marked-off distance.

When you're done, weigh the fertilizer you've caught in the pan, and multiply the width of the spreader by the distance you covered (in this case, 2 feet by 50 feet). The result is the square feet of coverage for the amount of fertilizer you weighed (100 square feet).

Now do the math. Say there was 1 pound of fertilizer in the pan. The spreader is dropping at a rate of 1 pound per 100 square feet. Now convert to the standard bag specification of 1,000 square

feet, and you get 10 pounds per 1,000 square feet (1/10 = 10/100). If this doesn't match the rate listed on the bag, adjust the setting on the spreader to account for the difference.

Calibrating a Broadcast Spreader

Fill the hopper of the spreader and begin spreading for a few feet along a parking lot or driveway. Measure the width of the spread material. Divide 1,000 (the standard distribution measure) by the width. This is your test distance. Now mark a test path measuring that distance. Fill the hopper with 5 pounds of material, and spread it along the test distance. Empty the remaining material in the hopper into a plastic grocery bag.

Weigh the bag and subtract the weight from 5 pounds. This is the figure for how much the spreader drops over 1,000 square feet. Check that amount against the figure on the bag, and adjust the spreader setting accordingly.

How to Spread Fertilizer

Adjust your spreader to the setting recommended by the fertilizer or seed manufacturer.

TIP: Put sand, crushed gravel or the actual fertilizer you'll use into the spreader and test it on a driveway or other hard surface. This will help you determine how fast to walk, and if the unit is distributing in a uniform pattern.

Clean Up Spillage ▶

Clean up any fertilizer that has been spilled or broadcast on hard surfaces such as sidewalks or driveways. Fertilizer left on these surfaces may be washed by rain into the edges of the lawn, causing those specific areas to go into a burst of growth. Even worse, rain or sprinkler overspray can wash loose fertilizer into a storm drain or other area where it can make its way into local water resources and the water table, where it can have an adverse effect on the ecosystem.

(continued)

Fill the spreader's hopper on the driveway or other hard surface, away from the lawn and any areas of vegetation.

Start spreading fertilizer along an outside edge of the lawn. Make sure you can see where the fertilizer is dropping. Repeat along the opposite edge.

Continue spreading fertilizer between and perpendicular to these two header strips. Hold the hopper gate closed as you make your turn at each end. Overlap passes by the width of a wheel.

Keep one wheel on the edge between the lawn and garden beds, tree rings, and other areas. When you have covered the entire lawn, water the surface thoroughly.

Topdressing Your Lawn

Although it is one of the simplest lawn-maintenance techniques, topdressing is also one of the most effective. A favorite practice of professional groundskeepers, it involves applying a layer of organic material to the top of the lawn and sifting it down to the soil. Topdressing can improve the soil without tearing up the sod. It works slowly to add organic material into the soil and create a more beneficial structure. The practice can also level out depressions in the lawn, as well as stimulate new growth to create a denser, more weed- and disease-resistant turf.

You can topdress with compost, although professionals often use a mix of three parts sand to three parts compost, mixed with one part sphagnum peat. The idea is the same no matter what material you're using: shovel a layer on top of the grass and get it to the soil.

To be effective, you should look to distribute around three pounds of the organic material per square yard. More is better, as long as none is left sitting on top of the grass where it could block sun and air and actually diminish growth in some areas. You can topdress at any time in the season, but the fall is best, especially after you have aerated the lawn.

Tools & Materials ▸

Wheelbarrow
Shovel
Garden rake
Spring rake

Garden fork
Compost or
  organic mix

How to Topdress the Lawn

Measure and mix the components of your topdressing (3 parts sand, 3 parts compost, 1 part peat moss is used here). Use a garden fork or spade to mix ingredients and break up any large pieces.

Shovel the mixture across the lawn evenly. You should distribute about 3 to 4 pounds of topdressing mix per square yard of lawn.

Rake out the mixture with the back and front of a garden rake, then use a spring rake to work the mix into the grass.

Mowing Fundamentals

It's a simple thing, cutting the grass. But it's also one of the most important things you'll do to your lawn, so you'll want to make sure to do it the right way. Mowing incorrectly exposes your lawn to disease and stress and, if nothing else, it just makes the lawn look bad—the exact opposite effect you're after by mowing in the first place.

Mowing is actually what separates "formal lawns" from wild fields of grass. By mowing, we prevent the plant from flowering and eventually growing seedheads. This keeps it in a perpetual state of growth until it gives up and shuts down in the face of the offseason. The quintessential lawn is one that is beautifully uniform and flat across its surface, like a dead-calm lake.

Mowers come in many types, sizes, and styles, and the one you pick will affect not only how comfortable you are as you mow, but also how quickly you can mow your lawn and how difficult the chore will be. You'll want to pick a mower based on the size of your yard, your budget, and the extra features such as mulching capability, that fit with the way you want to maintain your lawn.

How you use that mower is the other part of the equation. Carefully choosing the right mower height, the right time to mow, the right frequency, and the right method will all contribute to how well your lawn fights disease, crowds out weed growth, and thrives to grow as thick and full as possible. Of course, the result is also a terrific looking lawn that will be the envy of your neighbors.

Cordless, electric, or gas-powered, all lawnmowers are dangerous and demand that you always follow safe use recommendations.

Warning ▸

Lawnmowers are dangerous equipment with sharp blades and movements that can be unpredictable. One momentary lapse in concentration is all it takes for a mower to cause serious injury or worse. Mower safety should be commonsense, but the nearly 70,000 Americans who are injured every year in mower accidents belie that assumption. Observing simple safety guidelines will take much of the risk out of your lawn maintenance.

- Never disable safety features or remove the guards on a mower. If a feature is impairing the functional efficiency of the machine, you need to have a professional repair it. Period.
- Always take a moment to police the area you're mowing before you mow, to ensure that there are no hidden dangers, like rocks, bottles or pieces of glass, toys, or other debris.
- Allow any power mower to cool down for 30 minutes before cleaning or storing it.
- Children younger than 16 should not operate riding mowers, and children younger than 12 should not operate push mowers. More than 9,000 mower-related injuries each year happen to people younger than 18.
- All children should be off the lawn whenever you mow with a power mower. Adults should as well.
- Dress appropriately when mowing. Wear sturdy shoes, long pants, and eye protection.
- Never allow a passenger on a riding mower.
- Turn off the mower and allow a moment for the blades to stop moving before disengaging a bag attachment, clearing a discharge vent, or crossing a gravel surface.
- Do not handle gasoline or turn the mower on when it is still indoors. Refill the gas when the motor is cool, the mower is off, and it is sitting on a hard, level surface outdoors.
- Keep gas in an approved container. Clean up any spills immediately.
- Do not reverse a riding mower, or use one on a steep slope.
- Always keep all four wheels of a power mower on the ground. Do not tilt the front up for any reason.
- Do not use an electric mower if the cord is frayed or the wires are exposed.
- Avoid using power mowers in the rain.

Before You Mow

Before that all-important first mowing of the season, it's a good idea to take stock of your equipment and review your mowing practices. This is the perfect time to either tune-up and prepare your mower for a summer of action, or upgrade to a new, more efficient model. It's also the ideal moment to consider the way you mow and decide on a mowing schedule.

These considerations are not just about the health of your lawn. They also have to take into account local regulations and simple courtesy. This starts with the sound of the mower. As much as the sputter of a two-stroke mower engine evokes images of lazy Saturday afternoons, it's not so warm and fuzzy for everyone. If you're using a gas-powered mower, you'll be making a considerable amount of noise. Not surprisingly, people can be a little sensitive to the noise of a lawnmower. In fact, many homeowners' associations, and even some municipalities, have regulations governing at what times you can mow your lawn. Some experts even recommend wearing ear protection if your mower is exceptionally loud. But rules or not, mowing at a reasonable hour is just a matter of being a good neighbor.

You'll also need to decide what to do with the grass clippings. If you're only cutting the recommended one-third or less of the grass height, you can just leave the clippings on the lawn. They break down quickly and, depending on how much you've fed your lawn, the clippings can be a rich source of nitrogen. A mulching mower accelerates this process. Or, you can compost your clippings, unless you applied selective herbicides or pesticides, which could have a negative effect on the composting process.

If you don't want to compost your clippings, don't throw them away. Collect them in biodegradable bags and take them to the recycling or compost programs at the local sanitation or parks and recreation departments.

When to Mow ▸

All other considerations aside, as far as the lawn is concerned, some times are much better than others for mowing. The goal is to prevent damage to the grass blades and limit stress to the grass. The best times for this are in the early morning right after any dew has dried, but before the sun is at full strength, or in the early evening before it gets dark.

Other than those general guidelines, the actual days you choose to mow should be dictated by observing your lawn. Grass grows at different rates over the course of a season, depending on how much water it gets, how recently it has been fertilized (and what type of fertilizer was used), and other stress factors such as drought.

A good rule of thumb is to know the optimal height of your species of grass and always cut it when it grows a third more than that height. This may mean mowing twice in a week at some points, and once every ten days at others. Being flexible and responding to the needs of the grass is one of the ways you create a truly wonderful and visually appealing lawn.

Types of Lawnmowers

A lawnmower should be easy enough for you to use regularly, so that you'll never have a reason not to cut the lawn when it needs it. Your selection should be based on the amount of work you're comfortable doing (if you're in great shape, a reel mower or basic push mower may be right for you; if you have mobility issues or an extremely large lawn, you may need a riding mower) and other factors, such as how important the environmental impact of the machine is to you.

REEL MOWERS

The reel mower is the classic push mower, but it is no longer the heavy clunker of old. New versions are light, easy-to-use, and more height-adjustable than their predecessors. This is the environmentally friendly alternative to a power mower—not to mention being much quieter. The blades on a reel mower are mounted to spin clockwise around the axle between the wheels, passing by a sharp-edged cutting bar. The action is like scissors, and creates a distinctively clean cut. But it also accounts for the limitations; reel mowers can't be set to cut as high as power units, and they don't do well over a lawn with irregular terrain. Because the wheels box in the cutting cylinder, reel mowers cannot edge as closely as other types do to walls, fences and other vertical barriers. That translates to more clean-up work with a string trimmer or clippers. Power reel mowers are usually used only by professionals due to their high cost, but new cordless electric models are available for around $200. Just the same, the most popular types remain the contemporary lightweight push versions. They require some physical labor and are usually recommended for lawns less than 2,000 square feet. You'll also need to have the blades professionally sharpened, unless you're a skilled sharpener. These mowers come in standard cutting widths from 14 to 24 inches, and better models are adjustable from ½ to about 2½ inches high.

Reel mower

GAS-POWERED ROTARY WALK-BEHIND MOWERS

Although electric and cordless models have eaten into their market share, gas-powered mowers remain the most popular type. The mower comes equipped with a two-stroke or four-stroke engine; the two-stroke is noisier, less reliable, and pollutes more, while four-stroke models with overhead valves are more expensive. These mowers are built with cutting decks ranging from 18 to 22 inches wide, and can cut grass from 1 to over 4 inches high. Engine power differs based on the size of the unit, but manufacturers have largely stopped using horsepower as the standard, so you may need to compare models based on cubic inch displacement or torque ratings.

The blades spin horizontally, blowing the clippings into a rear or side bag, out through a side discharge vent, or around inside the deck and back down into the lawn (mulching action). Gas mowers require more maintenance than electric models, and filling a gas tank is less convenient than plugging in a cord or a rechargeable battery. You can, however, opt for a self-propelled model.

Lawn Size ▶

The size of your yard will factor into your mowing decision. Mowing a ¼ acre of lawn requires you to walk between 1 mile and 2 miles. If your yard is fairly small—from a few hundred sq. ft. to around ¼ acre—you can consider a reel mower, or either type of push power mower. A riding mower will be too great an investment for such a small lawn (unless you aren't physically capable of walking a mower). A medium size yard, from about ¼ to ½ acre is landscape that needs to be mowed with some sort of a power mower. An electric or gas mower—especially a self-propelled model—should be more than sufficient, although depending on the layout, you may want to consider a small riding mower. Beyond ½ acre, you either need a powered, self-propelled push mower with a large deck or, more likely, a riding mower.

You should also consider the topography of your yard. If your lawn covers a steep slope, a riding mower is not a great idea. If the surface itself is uneven, a reel mower is going to struggle to cut the tops of the blades evenly.

Walk-behind gas mower

ELECTRIC-POWERED PUSH MOWERS

These come in two versions: corded and cordless. Electric models with cords tend to be lighter, but rechargeable cordless versions don't entail the sometimes-cumbersome navigation around the cord. Cordless machines are equipped with detachable batteries that are recharged in a charger, or with fixed batteries that are just plugged in to a standard house outlet between mowings. Battery life—both between charges, and before needing replacement—is a key point to consider when shopping for a cordless model. Electric mowers were at one time considerably underpowered in relation to their gas-powered competitors. But manufacturers have made strides, and now the playing field is much more level. The blade technology is approximately the same, but the mowing swath of most electrics is generally narrower than that of comparable gas-powered units. If you're considering a corded model, make sure to check how long the extension cord can be before the amperage drops and the motor power decreases.

Battery-powered walk-behind mower

Corded electric lawnmower

RIDING MOWERS

A riding mower is a significant purchase because you're buying a vehicle. The whole idea is to make mowing a large yard—anything over ½ acre—easier and quicker. Riding mowers also accommodate those people who aren't capable of pushing a lawnmower. Expect to pay just under $1,000 for a basic model to well over $5,000 for a lawn tractor with all the bells and whistles. The price will depend primarily on the size and type of riding mower, and the features it comes with. You'll choose between a front- or rear-mounted engine; a rear engine makes it easier to scan the grass ahead while you mow, while a front-mounted engine offers more power. Zero-turn radius (ZTR) models offer the best of both worlds, but you'll pay a premium for them. A ZTR riding mower is a special type in which the rider sits in front of the engine and right on top of the mowing deck. This allows him or her to see better and take advantage of the extremely responsive and nimble steering system. The steering is controlled by levers and steering bars, and is designed to allow for precision cutting. It can save a lot of time over a traditional riding mower. A ZTR mower is a good choice for a very large lawn with many obstacles such as trees or beds. But be aware that it takes some manual dexterity to exploit the sensitive steering mechanism on this mower.

Deck widths range between 38 and 60 inches; as with other mowers, the larger the deck the quicker the mower will finish the job. There are also different drive systems, including hydrostatic systems, power wheels, and blades with pumped fluid, so there is no direct geared connection between motor and implement. Ultimately, riding mowers require more maintenance and are more expensive to operate than any other mower type.

Tractor vs. Mower ▶

If you're shopping for a riding mower, you're likely to come across models that are called "riding tractors." The difference is that a riding mower functions solely as a mower. A riding tractor, on the other hand, can be used with special attachments to dethatch, aerate, spread fertilizer, or topdress the lawn, and even plow snow. If you want to do all those things over a large area, consider going with a riding tractor.

Riding lawnmower/lawn tractor

Troubleshooting Your Lawnmower

Mowers are, for the most part, remarkably reliable. With just a little bit of regular maintenance, a gas or electric model can easily last a decade or more, providing excellent service all the while. But sometimes even the most reliable machines have problems. When that happens to your mower, you need to diagnose the situation to determine if it's an easy fix you can do at home, or if you're going to need to make a trip to the local repair shop.

MOWER IS VIBRATING WHEN RUNNING

This is a sign of a serious problem and no mower should be used when it is noticeably vibrating. It's likely that you've run over an object and your mower blade is damaged, which can cause it to become unbalanced and throw off the operation of the whole machine. Turn off the mower and disconnect the power source, and then turn it over and inspect the blade. If the blade is the cause of the vibration, it will be visually deformed or cracked all the way through. Replace the blade.

If your gas mower won't start, look for a fuel shut-off switch and make sure it is not in the open position.

Warning ▸

Whenever you are investigating a problem with a lawnmower, regardless of what type it is, the mower must be completely shut off and disengaged. That means removing the battery or unplugging an electric mower, disconnecting the spark plug wire from a gas push mower, and removing the key entirely from a riding mower. It should go without saying that if you are having problems with a safety feature such as a guard that is bent and interfering with the operation of the mower, or a dead man's switch that is cutting out, have them repaired immediately.

THE MOWER WON'T START

Begin by checking the most obvious causes first. For an electric mower, check that the cord is plugged securely into the outlet, and that power is flowing to the outlet. If neither of those is the cause, check the fuse controlling the outlet, and then check the mower cord for a break or damage that would interrupt the power to the mower.

If your mower is cordless, check that the battery is installed correctly in the mower. Then, determine if the battery is charged, and if it is holding its charge (see photo, below).

Gas mowers—push or riding—can fail to start for many different reasons. Check that you have gas in the tank and that it is fresh. Drain and replace the gas if you know it has been in the tank for more than one month, or if you're in doubt as to how old it is. Check that the spark plug wire is securely attached, and that the spark plug itself is clean and correctly gapped. Check that the battery cables are tight and clean and, if they are, test the battery to determine if it is still holding a charge. On a riding mower specifically, make sure that the blades are not engaged, in which case a safety feature would prevent the engine from starting. If you have a high-end, late-model riding mower, there may be a problem with the seat sensor, so that it doesn't register that anybody is in the seat—another safety feature that will prevent starting.

Changing Cutting Height ▸

Depending on the model and age of your mower, setting the wheel height adjustment on a push mower can be a difficult, strength-testing feat. To make it easier with any mower, use a scrap 4 × 4 or the sidewalk curb to prop the deck up, so that the back wheels are off the ground (this only works with rear-wheel height-adjustment models), then change the height adjustment. It should require far less pressure to make the change.

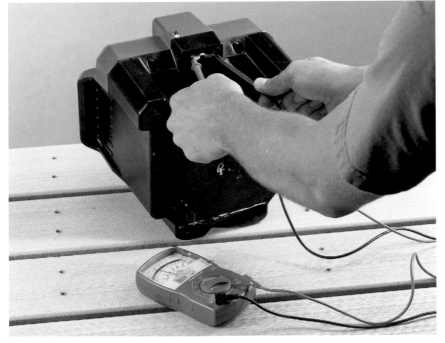

Cordless electric mower batteries can only be recharged so many times before they can no longer hold the charge. A quick test of the battery will determine if it needs replacement. You can do this yourself with an ohmmeter, or take it to a service station.

Lawnmower Maintenance

Given how much engineering goes into name-brand mowers these days, there's simply no reason your mower shouldn't last many, many years, if not decades. That's partly up to you; if you perform all the regular maintenance your machine requires (or pay to have it performed), you give your mower its best shot at longevity. Gas mowers require the most regular maintenance.

- Perform an oil change at least once a year and according to the manufacturer's directions (many riding mowers have an hour meter that logs hours used for maintenance purposes). Whenever you change the oil, change the filter. To ensure against leaks, coat your finger with fresh oil and rub it along the rubber gasket on the oil filter before replacing the filter. Always use the oil recommended by the manufacturer.
- Replace the engine's spark plug annually, even if your owner's manual doesn't call for it.
- Replace the air filter every two years unless the manufacturer calls for more frequent changes, or if the filter becomes clogged.
- Make sure gas is fresh. All too often, homeowners keep a can of gas around for months or even years. Old gas gathers impurities and its octane content diminishes. Not only does this mean the engine will run more poorly, it can also damage all the parts of the engine the gas touches.
- If you own a riding mower, you'll also need to check the drive belt for wear on a regular basis, and replace it when it is worn.
- When you're putting the mower up for the winter, drain all the fluids and empty your gas can. Put the gas you drain and gas in the can into your car's fuel tank, preferably when the tank is more than half full. Recycle the oil at a local gas station.
- **Electric mowers:** About the only thing you'll need to worry about is the battery on a cordless mower. Always check the cord on a cord mower, and if you find any nicks or splits, replace the cord.

Use a stiff bristle brush to clean cooling fins and other engine parts after removing the blower housing.

Store gas in a proper, approved container, and add leftover gas to your car regularly, so that the gas doesn't go stale.

Caring for Mower Blades

The blade is an incredibly important part of the mower. If the blade is in poor condition, it can affect your entire lawn. And the negative effects aren't just related to appearance. A ragged top cut on a leaf of grass opens the grass plant up to disease. That's why keeping your lawnmower blade sharp is the first line of defense against lawn diseases.

Sharpening your blade is a simple task that should be done at least once every season (and it certainly doesn't hurt to do it more than once). Before you inspect for nicks or other obvious damage, clean the blade with a wire brush. Serious dents, cracks, or deep nicks in the blade mean it's probably time for a replacement blade. If you can't remove the nick fairly easily during the sharpening process, you'll need to replace the blade.

As part of your regular cleanings, consider treating the blade metal with a rust remover to remove any oxidation, and a rust retardant to stop it from coming back. You can find a number of these products at hardware stores and large home centers.

Always take your time when you balance the blade because an imbalanced blade can cause engine damage or damage to the underside of the deck. Use care when you reattach the blade; some models are only meant to go in one direction. A torque wrench is the best tool to use for tightening the nut that secures your mower blade. Follow the inch–pounds recommendation from the blade manufacturer as your guide.

Tools & Materials ▸

Closed-end wrench
Torque wrench
10" file
Vise

Mower blade
Hammer
Nail
Gloves

Mulching Adapter Kits ▸

When it comes time to replace your lawnmower blade, you have an opportunity to upgrade your standard push mower. Manufacturers make mulching adapter kits to turn a standard mower into a mulching mower. Standard mowers cut grass blades and then blow the clippings out the discharge into a bag or down onto the lawn, where the pieces may take some time to decompose. Mulching action recirculates the clippings under the deck so that they can be cut several times before being blown down into the lawn. Mulching kits are not made for all makes and models of mowers, but it's certainly worth checking with your local lawnmower retailer. The kits range from about $40 to over $200 depending on the model and size mower you are converting. They usually include a subhousing that is installed under the deck, new blades, and new hardware. Installation is fairly easy and it just might save you bagging your clippings the next time you mow.

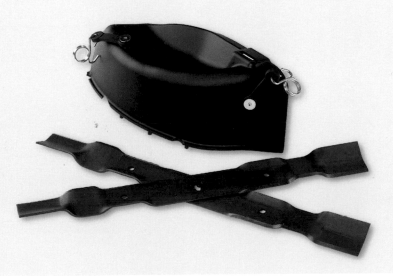

How to Sharpen a Mower Blade

Remove the spark plug or battery from the mower, or otherwise disable it so that it cannot accidentally start. Tip the mower on its side, so that the entire underdeck area is accessible. *Tip: If your fuel tank contains gasoline, remove the cap, cover the opening with foil or plastic wrap (inset), and then replace the cap. This prevents gas from dripping out of the vent hole in the cap.*

Wedge a wood scrap piece between the blade and the mower deck to stabilize the blade so it doesn't spin while you remove the bolt holding it in place. You can also purchase a special device for this purpose from yard and garden centers.

Remove the blade. Use a closed-end wrench to loosen the bolt that secures the blade to the mower motor. If the bolt is stuck, try spraying it with penetrating lubricant and letting it soak in for a few minutes before retrying.

Secure the blade in a vise. Inspect the entire blade for damage, and then file along the cutting edge, using smooth, even strokes at an angle that matches the existing bevel. Use the same number of strokes on each edge.

5

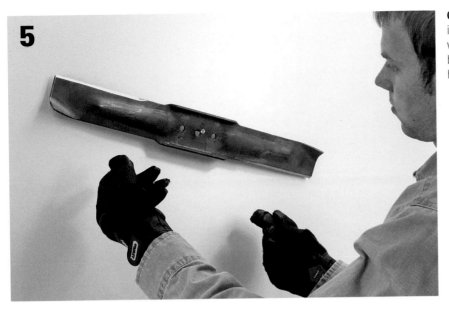

Check the blade's balance by hanging it on a nail that has been driven into the wall. The blade should hang level. If the blade is not balanced, file metal off the heavier end until it is.

6

Reattach the blade to the mower's motor following the manufacturer's instructions and cut a small strip of grass as a test. Inspect the tops of the cuttings to make sure they have been sliced cleanly, indicating that the blade is sharp.

Blade Balancing Cones ▸

Balancing a mower blade is an important last step before you reinstall the blade on the mower. There are a number of ways to accomplish this. If you don't feel comfortable hanging the blade on a nail and judging it on the wall, you can lock a screwdriver horizontally in the vise and slide the blade onto the shaft. But if you want to do it as the pros do it, buy a blade-balancing cone at your hardware store or lawnmower retailer. You simply sit these on a flat, level surface, slide the blade on top, and check the balance. The device is inexpensive and pretty much foolproof.

Mowing the Lawn

Mowing is traumatic to a grass plant, but you can mitigate the trauma by making wise choices about when and how to mow your lawn.

The benchmark of a good mowing job is a clean cut. The top of the blade should be sheared off as if you'd cut it with sharp scissors, not torn and ragged. There are many ways to avoid a poor cut, but they all start with maintaining your lawnmower, and using the mower correctly. Keep your lawnmower blade sharp. Although sharpening is recommended once a season, if you know your species of grass is famous for being tough and dense, or if it seems like the mower blade has taken a lot of abuse in confrontations with tree roots, small branches, rocks, or other obstacles, a mid-seasoning sharpening may be in order. You should also avoid mowing when the grass is wet. Wet grass rarely cuts cleanly or evenly, and it strains your lawnmower's engine as well, as grass sticks to the blades and the housing. Always clean the underside of the deck after mowing. The deck is engineered to create an airflow that draws grass blades upright so that they can be cut cleanly. If that airflow is blocked, the mower will cut less efficiently. The mower is also designed to cut while moving forward, not backward.

Mow the lawn according to its needs, not your convenience. Cut no more than a third of the blade height—it's actually a good idea to measure the grass so you know how tall it should be and when to cut it. The last cut of the season, however, should be slightly lower than the proper height for your grass. In times of drought, cut the grass higher than normal to help limit transpiration and conserve water in the soil. *Tip: A simple and useful trick for knowing when to cut the lawn is to match the optimal grass height to a corresponding height on your shoes or boots.*

A well-tended lawn is beautiful to behold and, if it's been mowed correctly, it's as healthy as it is good-looking.

Mowing on a Slope ▸

Slopes are challenges for every aspect of lawn care, but no more so than for mowing. If you own a riding mower, the best advice is not to use it on a slope, instead cutting that part of the lawn with a push mower. If you absolutely have to use a riding mower on a slope, the Outdoor Power Equipment Institute and the US Consumer Safety Product Commission both recommend that you ride the mower up and down, never across the slope. Although some professionals suggest mowing on the diagonal, that's every bit as dangerous as riding a mower across the slope.

In the case of a push mower, you should do the opposite: push it across the slope. The idea is to avoid pushing up the slope, where the mower might accidentally roll back onto your feet.

Fixing Mowing Mistakes ▸

None of us are perfect, and mowing isn't a perfect science. Sometimes life creeps up on you and your lawn has grown to a mini-jungle before you realize it. Or maybe you weren't paying attention to that big dip in your yard and you gave a spot of your lawn a crewcut instead of its usual 2 inches. Don't fret; those are fixable errors.

- **Cutting overgrown grass.** The secret here is not to shock the roots by lopping off a large portion of their food-producing top growth all at once. If you need to cut the grass height by ½, cut the first ¼ and then let the grass rest for a day or two. Then cut the other ¼ and you'll have prevented any undue stress to the grass plant.

- **Repairing a scalp.** A one-time event is traumatic but constant scalping can have a devastating impact, creating large bare patches. You'll need to fix the underlying problem that caused the scalp in the first place. But in the moment, feed the scalped area with calcium, manganese, and iron, and then water deeply. Continue to give that part of the lawn a daily watering for the next week or so. Within a couple of weeks it should be back to normal.

How to Mow the Right Way

Check the lawn for obstacles such as rocks or sticks. Adjust the height of the mower to the optimal height for your grass type (but never cut more than ⅓ of the total height).

Choose your direction. You should vary the direction of mowing each time you mow to prevent tire ruts. Start mowing along an outside edge.

Mowing Heights by Species ▸

COLD SEASON GRASSES

Kentucky Bluegrass	2–3"
Perennial Rye	2–3"
Tall Fescue	2½–3"
Creeping Bent Grass	¼–¾"

TRANSITION GRASSES

Buffalo	2–3"
Blue Grama	2–3"

WARM-SEASON GRASSES

Bahia	2–3"
Bermuda	¾–1½"
Centipede	1½–2"
St. Augustine	2–3"
Zoysia	1½–2"

Leave a buffer of an inch or two between the mower deck and the base of trees and shrubs. Be careful not to scalp the grass where roots have made the ground uneven. Overlap rows by a couple inches on each pass. This will ensure that you don't cut the grass unevenly. Check for any missed spots after you've mowed the entire lawn.

Clean the underside of the mower deck immediately after every use. For optimal mower performance and ideal cutting, the deck needs to be free and clear of clippings and other organic matter. *Tip: Help keep it clean by spraying a layer of cooking spray on the freshly cleaned underside. The spray will stop clippings from sticking and will keep the underside of the deck cleaner, longer.*

Variation: If you're using a reel mower, you usually need to overlap rows with a little more to spare because the cutting area doesn't reach as close to the mower tires as it does on most power mowers.

Mowing Patterns in the Lawn

Mowing patterns in your lawn is a simple way to add an interesting graphic element to your landscape. A basic design such as stripes in two directions is a good way to get acquainted with what it will take to create a more complicated pattern. Although they aren't difficult to achieve, take your time; the most successful patterns require a certain amount of precision.

Once you've done a basic stripe pattern, you can graduate to increasingly complex designs, such as a checkerboard or diagonal diamond pattern. Regardless of the pattern, the idea is the same: mow in the directions for the pattern you're trying to create, then roll the lawn in the same directions to bend the grass blades in that direction. The bent blades reflect light as a different color, creating the visual pattern.

It may seem impossible to do patterns if you have cut-ins and unusual shapes due to lawn beds or features such as trees. But for diagramming, consider the shape a square or rectangle; in mowing and rolling you'll just continue the pattern on the other side of the obstacle. You may have to use stakes and a string line to keep your rows straight.

Regardless of the pattern, it's always a good idea to put it down on paper before you put it on the lawn. Measure your lawn and lawnmower (wheel edge to wheel edge) and then layout the pattern on the page.

If the pattern goes horribly wrong, you can always roll the entire lawn in one direction to essentially "erase" your attempt. But no matter what pattern you use, or how it turns out, do not repeat the same pattern every time you mow or you'll damage the health of your grass.

Tools & Materials ▸

Lawnmower
Drum roller

Pencil and paper

Creating a dynamic lawn pattern is one way to make your lawn—and your home—stand out in the neighborhood.

How to Mow a Pattern

Begin by mowing a stripe in one direction. Mow as straight as possible. If your mower is self-propelled, control the direction carefully. Mow in the direction you'll be viewing the lawn, usually the width of the lawn.

At the end of each row, lift the front wheels up and carefully turn the mower around so that the outside wheels are aligned with the inside wheel strip from the previous row. Make a return pass in the opposite direction, keeping the wheels aligned carefully.

Continue mowing rows in alternating directions. When you're done, roll each row with a drum roller in the same direction the row was mowed.

Variation: To create a checkerboard pattern, complete all of your parallel rows and then repeat the process by cutting parallel rows that are perpendicular to the first passes. Roll the new rows in the same direction as they were cut.

Trimming & Edging

A perfectly manicured lawn cannot have sloppy borders. Even the lushest, deepest expanse of green grass will look shaggy and unfinished if it's growing out over sidewalks and paths, or if tufts of grass are rising up the sides of planter boxes and terraces. To give your lawn a look that truly says "finished," you must edge and trim it properly.

These are not back-breaking lawn-care tasks, but they do require attention to detail. To make everything go more smoothly, choose the right tool for the job. Edges can be cut sharply and crisply with a manual edger or a gas or electric power unit. Trimming where the mower can't reach can be accomplished with manual or electric shears. For bigger jobs, turn to the greater power of gas or electric string trimmers. Manual edgers and shears are fine for cleaning up a small lawn with straight borders. But for larger yards, you'll probably want to turn to a power model. There are many power edgers to choose from and most are easy and quick to use. Whichever tool you use, work slowly and steadily to avoid mistakes.

Warning ▶

When using power edgers and trimmers, wear long thick pants, sturdy shoes, gloves, and safety glasses, and follow these guidelines:

STRING TRIMMERS
- Use only the recommended size line.
- Before refilling a gas trimmer's tank, turn off the engine and let it cool.
- Never check a jam or problem with the trimmer head until the unit is completely disengaged.

POWER EDGERS
- Don't use a power edger next to a gravel path.
- If the edger strikes an object such as a buried rock, stop the unit and turn it off, and inspect for damage before continuing.

Trimming overgrown shrubs is related to the general lawn trimming routine—you need to cut back shrubs that shade out parts of the lawn, or that force pedestrians to walk off a path and onto the lawn to get around the projecting branches.

Well-mulched evergreen beds should be crisply separated from the lawn. The bed here is bordered with nearly invisible black plastic edging that is positioned several inches deep to prevent grass from migrating into the bed.

Hard edging, such as the inlaid bricks along the curved border of this patio, are the most effective and low-maintenance way to keep lawn edges neat and trim.

Choosing Trimming Tools

Aside from budget, your chief concerns in picking a trimmer for your lawn care should be how comfortable it is to use and how big your yard is. If you aren't able to bend down or kneel for more than a few minutes, manual trimmers aren't for you at all. If you've decided on a power trimmer, pick one that you can easily handle and control.

GRASS SHEARS

These were the weapon of choice before power trimmers came along, and they kept the borders of many a suburban lawn neat and tidy. Early versions were stiff to use and frequently led to arm, wrist, and hand fatigue. Newer models are lighter in weight, with padded ergonomic handles, smooth cutting action, and carbon steel blades that hold their edge for years. Top-of-line models can even cut through sod.

Long-neck grass shears are a special type in which cutting blades are separated from the handles by an extension pole that alleviates the need for the operator to bend down. *Tip: shop at the high end of the price range and you'll be rewarded with an ergonomically superior tool that causes fewer hand cramps and works more smoothly.*

ELECTRIC GARDEN SHEARS

Powered shears are a step up from hand-held grass shears in the ease-of-use department. Normally battery operated, these cordless tools are designed with ergonomic handles and balanced bodies that are comfortable to hold for extended periods. They are offered with interchangeable heads, giving you the ability to switch to small hedge trimmers as the need arises. The best models include an LED battery-life indicator and wide cutting heads. One of the big advantages of a powered version over the manual style is that it is easy to hold the cutter level to cut grass even with the grass cut by the lawnmower. They are also an environmentally friendly solution. You can even find an attachment pole to use these as long-handled grass shears.

Long-neck grass shears

Grass clippers

Cordless grass clippers

POWERED STRING TRIMMERS

Whether gas, electric, or cordless, string trimmers have similar ergonomic features. Look for the most comfortable grip for your hand, because how well you control the direction and motion of the trimmer head has a direct effect on the appearance of your trim job, as well as how safe the unit is for you to operate. You'll also have to decide between a tool with a curved or a straight shaft. Straight-shaft trimmers are great for tall people, and usually give better access to hard-to-reach areas. Trimmers with curved shafts are lighter and easier to handle.

GAS-POWERED STRING TRIMMERS

Gas-powered string trimmers are notoriously loud and they're heavy polluters. Recently, manufacturers have made some strides—prodded by legislation—to increase the efficiency and decrease the exhaust of their engines. A four-stroke engine is quieter and leaner than a two-stroke, but it is also heavier, making the trimmer harder to maneuver and more fatiguing. Consider the horsepower ratings and compare them to what you need to do. Do you cut thick-stalked weeds? Go with a powerful motor. For the average yard, you won't go wrong with a low or medium horsepower rating. Either way, the unit can operate continuously for a much longer time than most cordless electric units, with more power to burn. Any gas-powered trimmer will, however, require tune-ups and maintenance. Ask about the starting procedure for any trimmer you're considering, because some start much easier than others. Translucent fuel tanks are also a good idea, so you can see where you are with gas at a glance.

ELECTRIC STRING TRIMMERS

The electric trimmer category includes both cordless (battery powered) and corded models. Corded models are encumbered by a power cord, and most now have some sort of cord control or lock system on the handle. When considering different units, keep in mind that a trimmer with the motor mounted near the handle will be easier to use than one with the motor mounted at the head. A swivel head is a handy feature that makes edging with the trimmer a simple job. Unit to unit you'll want to compare battery charge life, overall weight, and voltage. The power is much better than it once was, but electric trimmers still can't compare head-to-head with gas-powered units in this category. Technology has improved and battery chargers on some models can charge the battery in as little as an hour, and batteries last longer than they once did. However, they remain a much greener option than any gas model.

Gas-powered
string trimmer

Cordless (battery powered)
string trimmer

Choosing an Edger

Lawn edgers are used to cut a nice, crisp border around grassy areas. The available options are similar to trimmer choices; you'll find manual and power versions, with the powered tool running on gas or electric (both corded and cordless). Edgers are somewhat more specialized than other outdoor equipment types, and the needs of your yard should figure first and foremost in your decision of which model to buy.

MANUAL EDGERS

There are two types of manual edgers: step-on and rotary. The most common example of a step-on edger is the half-moon edger, with its namesake cutting blade and a small lip above it for the user's foot. These require a certain amount of effort and force to use effectively, and it helps if you are bigger and stronger than the average person. In any case, they would be very tiresome to use for any but a lawn with limited edges to cut. Half-moon edgers function like shovels, so your primary interest when selecting (and maintaining) one should be the blade. It should be hardened steel, and the bigger the crescent, the better. Rotary edgers are somewhat easier to use. They feature a toothed cutter mounted to the side of a wheel (or wheels) that guides the cutter along the lawn. These are fairly efficient and, although they require a little elbow grease, are easy to use. If you're shopping for rotary edgers, look for cushioned grips and extra wide guide wheels, as well as self-cleaning features for the cutting wheel.

Half-moon edger

Rotary edger

Gas-powered edger

ELECTRIC EDGERS

As with electric trimmers, electrically powered edgers come in both corded and cordless versions. The corded models often come with a handle-mounted cord control. But battery-powered, cordless models are the more popular. Manufacturers are steadily ramping up the power and running time of these machines. A newer, high-end model will do a great job of edging through even tough dense turf. Some edgers can be converted to a landscape trencher for digging out small trenches. As with the trimmers, battery-charging time has been reduced and use time has been increased. Look for a model that is comfortable, well balanced and that you can get your weight behind.

GAS-POWERED EDGERS

The same drawbacks that apply to the small gas-powered engines on trimmers and other yard equipment apply to gas-powered edgers. Even modern two-stroke edger engines are loud and fairly inefficient, although four-stroke engines are more reliable—and the added weight usually isn't an issue with an edger. Gas-powered edgers range from modest units that look something like trimmers with a cutting wheel mounted vertically, to top-end edgers that resemble small lawnmowers, with two wide—or even four—wheels and a powerful engine. More powerful edgers are easier to move along, and offer the ability to cut turf for other landscape projects such as defining and cutting out a bed in the middle of a lawn. If you have a large lawn with edged borders on at least three sides, one of these high-end units may be the right choice. But if you have a more modest lawn, look for a smaller unit with a single guide wheel and single shaft handle.

Electric edger tool (corded)

Trimming Your Lawn

Trimming is a finishing touch to mowing your lawn. You are simply cutting those areas the mower can't reach, such as grass around trees and fences. Try to cut the grass as closely as possible to the way the mower cuts. When you're trimming with a string trimmer, concentrate on keeping the head of the trimmer at the same level the grass was mowed. You can, however, use a slight downward angle to improve sightlines.

It takes a lot of concentration to cut clean level lines with a string trimmer, but don't lose sight of safety issues. A trim line spins at a high speed and it can catch rocks, small toys, and other yard debris, flinging them a long way at a high speed. Keep an eye out for any surprises hidden at the borders of the lawn, and don't trim when there are children present.

Your lawn will look its best—and you'll keep the grass at the fringes as healthy as possible—if you trim every time you mow, regardless of whether the lawn appears to need trimming. As an extension of mowing, trimming has to follow the same rules; you don't want to take off more than ⅓ of the height of the grass you trim if you can help it. You can also use the trimmer for light edging work, basically to square up light overgrowth. Simply turn the machine so the head is vertical (some units have swivel heads for just this purpose).

Finish up trimming by checking the trimmer head and housing for any debris or damage. Replace the spool or wire if necessary; there are several different types, so follow the manufacturer's directions and replace like with like.

A string trimmer is an effective tool for trimming grass in areas around your yard where a lawnmower cannot reach.

Clean up: Trimming is all about looking neat and tidy, so you don't want to leave clippings laying around loose. A quick pass with a cordless blower/vacuum will suck up any loose clippings and keep the house and lawn looking sharp.

Using a String Trimmer

Before you start, inspect the trimmer for any damage and determine if the string needs to be replaced. For electric trimmers, inspect the trimmer's power cord to make sure it is in good condition—the cord casing often is damaged accidentally by the trimmer string.

To trim edges and vertical spots such as along edging or next to a wall, angle the head of the trimmer slightly downward toward the surface. Trim slowly and steadily in a line.

To mow small areas that the lawnmower cannot reach, keep the trimming head level at the same height as you mow the grass, and methodically cut all the grass in the area.

Option: You can edge with a string trimmer by holding the head at a 90° angle to the ground. Carefully move along parallel to the line you are edging. Because the trim head and string will be exposed, make certain there are no people or animals nearby, and wear eye protection.

Edging Your Lawn

Turfgrass doesn't honor borders. It grows where it wants to grow, and edgers slice through it to make a clean edge. Lawn edgers actually come in handy all around the lawn. The traditional use is to provide a crisp edge and cut through grass overgrowth sprawling onto sidewalks, paths, driveways, and other surfaces bordering the lawn. But edgers prove much more useful than just keeping straight lines shipshape. They can also be used to cut through the surface along the proposed new edge of a garden bed. In that sense, they help to outline the borders of your lawn, no matter what you put on the other side.

Using an edger is a relatively straightforward affair. The crudest types are simply step-on tools with a blade that looks like a shovel blade that has been squashed flat. Lips line the top of the blade so that you can step on it, pushing the blade down into the soil and cutting the edge. It's a lot of work to edge a long border this way. That work can be cut down by using a rotary edger, although these are meant for light edging along driveways or preexisting surfaces, not cutting new edges for garden beds or around tree rings.

For the full range of edging tasks, most homeowners turn to power edgers, either gas-powered types, or electric models like the one we show here.

A good cordless edger will do just about everything you need an edger to do, and in an ecologically mindful way. Most are capable of cutting a new edge through existing lawn, and are quick and easy to work with.

Gas-powered edgers require the same kind of follow-up maintenance that gas-powered mowers do. Electric edgers are pretty much maintenance free, although you will have to replace the blade when it starts to wear out or loses a battle with a rock or piece of cement that has hidden under a dirt edge. Otherwise, since edging only needs to be done once every few weeks to keep everything looking great, your edger should last a long, long time.

An edger creates neat borders around your lawn, especially where it meets sidewalks and pathways. You can use hand egdging tools, but for larger yards you'll want to invest in a gas-powered, electric, or cordless edger.

How to Edge a Lawn

Check the area to be edged for rocks, large sticks, or any other debris. Make sure your edger is in good running condition, with no major nicks on the blade.

Align the edger and, holding the blade up off the surface, start the motor and allow the blade to reach full speed. Then gently lower it to begin edging.

Edge slowly following the line of the sidewalk or other guide, paying close attention to avoid any buried rocks or obstructions such as sprinkler heads.

Score Cutting Lines ▶

Use your power edger to make straight cuts through your turf before beginning an excavation. The edger creases a neat border so the sod you remove or turf you dig out leaves a clean line in the lawn.

How to Replace a String Trimmer Spool

Unplug the trimmer, remove the battery, or disconnect the spark plug if the trimmer is a gas-powered model. Place the unit on a workbench, with the bottom facing up.

Press the release tabs on the spool hub cover and pull it off. Lift the spool out from the spool hub, and clear any line or debris from around the hub housing.

Insert the end of the line on the new spool into the eyelet in the hub. Pull the line through the hole, maintaining tension as you drop the new spool into place in the hub, with the notched side exposed.

Alternative: To use bulk line rather than a replacement spool, insert one end of the line through the spool's hole and hold it as you pull the rest of the line through the slot and wind the line in the direction of the arrow on the spool.

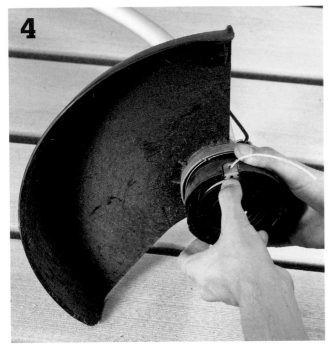

Press down on the spool gently and rotate it until you feel it drop into position. It should still be able to turn slightly to the left and right. Replace the hub cover and reconnect the power source for the trimmer.

Field-test the trimmer to make sure the new string is feeding correctly.

How to Replace a Power Edger Blade

Make sure the edger is disconnected from its power source (unplugged or with the battery removed). Prop the blade guard in the open position to expose the blade and blade housing. Immobilize the blade against a wood scrap to keep it from moving while you loosen the blade mounting nut with a wrench. Remove the blade, noting the position of the inner and outer spacers.

Set the blade spacer over the arbor bolt and then slide the new blade into place over the spacer. Replace the mounting nut and tighten it down with a wrench. Close the housing door and lock it down by turning the knob.

Water & Your Lawn

Your lawn can live with a deficiency of any nutrient or mineral. It can struggle along through overcast days with minimal sunlight. It can even fight through clay soil with amazingly small amounts of air. But it cannot live without water.

How much water the lawn requires, and when it needs it, are critically important issues if the grass is going to thrive. Understanding those needs starts with understanding how the plant uses water.

Grass plants bring in water through their roots. But the moisture doesn't stay for long. The plant consumes water in the process of photosynthesis, as it breaks down carbohydrates for energy. Like us, grass plants increase their metabolic processes in warm weather. Unless the temperature gets so hot that the grass plant actually goes dormant, the hotter and drier the weather, the more water it will need to stay healthy. As the weather warms, photosynthesis increases and the plant consumes an increasing amount of water. Add to that the fact that water is lost out of individual blades in a process similar to human sweating, called transpiration. This process actually keeps blades upright and strong, but it means water is constantly moving up through the plant and out through the leaves.

Roots will grow far to find all the necessary water for the plant to grow strong. How far, thick, and healthy they grow depends in no small part on how often and in what amounts water is available. Think back to the initial examination of your lawn and the soil structure in side view; you'll remember that healthy roots form a network that travels down inches, spreading out as it goes.

A spread and depth like that shows that the roots are growing deep in search of water, and they are finding enough to fuel the plant and grow denser roots.

Soil Situation ▶

The type of soil you have is going to affect water drainage and, ultimately, how you need to deliver water. As you recall, how well a soil holds onto water and nutrients depends on how much sand, loam, or clay makes up the soil. If you think about it, it makes sense. A sandy soil drains quickly, while heavy, dense clay soil is going to be slow to absorb any moisture at all. To give you some idea of the real-time effects of different soil types, here's how long it will take ½" of water to soak down about 8" in each type.

Sandy Soil:	30 min.
Loamy Soil:	1 hour
Clay Soil:	2½ hours

Water that simply sits on grass blades is useless to the plant because plant leaves are not equipped to absorb moisture. Only the plant's underground root system can draw in water, so the point of watering your lawn is to saturate the dirt.

On the other hand, if you were to look at a side view of the root structure in a lawn that has been watered frequently and briefly, you'd see shallow roots spread out underneath the plants. The roots don't need to grow far down in search of water because it's always there. Root growth is retarded in this instance, affecting uptake of nutrients and resulting in scraggly top growth. Roots of grass plants suffering from a lack of moisture are likely going to stretch down in their search for water, but the structure and density are greatly diminished from those of a healthy plant and, once again, top growth will be limp and far less robust than in a healthy lawn.

So effective watering involves both depth and frequency. Watering more deeply and less frequently (once or twice a week) is much better for lawn health than more frequent, shallow waterings. If your automatic sprinkler system is set to water every day, you're not doing your lawn any favors. Lawn watering is also affected by many different variables including soil texture, weather, conditions such as compaction, and other factors. Giving the lawn the proper amount of water involves monitoring and understanding these conditions, and choosing the proper time, method, and amount of lawn irrigation.

The average lawn needs about 1 inch of water every week when it is not dormant. It can get that water from rain or from you. Warm-season grasses will, in general, be okay with less. Cool-season grasses in dry arid regions may need slightly more. But the 1 inch rule is a good baseline.

Gauging Rain ▸

Accurately gauging how much moisture your lawn receives from rain is essential to adjusting how much you should water the lawn—overwatering can be as bad as letting the lawn go thirsty. A simple, inexpensive way to monitor the exact amount of rainfall is a rain gauge, a small plastic basin that you stick in the lawn in an inconspicuous spot. You can also use the gauge to determine how much water your sprinklers or sprinkler system are delivering to the lawn, which will help you decide when to dial back or ramp up watering.

Rainfall is one of the trickier variables you'll need to account for in determining the best watering schedule for your lawn. Note that areas of high runoff, such as space around downspouts, should require less watering. The trick is to be aware of how your yard holds water and to pay attention to accumulation amounts.

Conserving Water

Conserving water is an issue that most homeowners must deal with sooner or later. Whether you want to live green and help the environment, or just lessen the pain of your summer water bills, water conservation is a continuing and pressing concern. And all indicators suggest it will become even more important in the coming decades.

If you have a cool-season lawn, you'll need to decide whether you want to let it go dormant in the summer heat—its natural state—or if you want to keep it green by using precious resources to artificially hydrate the grass. Dormancy is not death. It's simply a state where the grass turns brown and goes metabolically inactive. If your region or local municipality is under water restrictions, this is the environmentally responsible thing to do, and local regulations may require you do it. Keep in mind that even a dormant lawn needs some water—about ¼" every other week.

If you aren't under a water restriction, or if you're growing a highly drought-tolerant, warm-weather species, you should still look to optimize the water you use. Water the lawn early in the morning (5 or 6 a.m. is ideal) before the sun is at full force, to give the water time to soak into the soil. Although some experts recommend watering at night to avoid evaporation, the reality is that wet grass that doesn't completely dry before dark becomes an excellent breeding ground for diseases.

You also want to take into account your grass species—which may need much less than the average 1 inch per week (see graphic below). When in doubt, look for the telltale signs that a grass is struggling with a lack of moisture. These include a bluish-gray cast to the overall lawn, inward folding blades, and footprints that remain when someone walks across the lawn.

Which brings up the last part of the water conservation puzzle. The less you stress the lawn, the better it will handle any kind of drought conditions, modest or severe. Although you can't put a giant umbrella over your lawn during a string of hot days, you can keep kids and pets off the lawn, and forego fertilizing. Feeding a lawn during a drought period causes it to try to grow, using more water than it normally would use, and stressing the grass when it can't find those water reserves.

Weather-Aware Watering ▸

Your watering schedule should be adapted to many different factors, not the least of which is the weather.

You can pull back on your watering when the weather turns cloudy and overcast, when temperatures drop, or there's little wind and high humidity. And, of course, you should always take into account the amount of rain that has recently fallen.

Water more frequently when the grass has been subjected to long periods of intense, direct sunlight, high winds, dry conditions, and warmer-than-normal temperatures.

GRASS THIRST BY SPECIES

MORE   LESS

Kentucky Bluegrass   Creeping Bentgrass   Tall Fescue   Perennial Ryegrass   Centipede Grass   St. Augustine   Zoysia   Bermuda Buffalo

Alternative Sources for Lawn Water

Watering the lawn does not always mean turning on the hose or activating the in-ground sprinkler system. As water has become a scarce commodity in many of the more crowded and warmer parts of the country, alternatives to the traditional sources of lawn water are enjoying increasing popularity.

The first of these is the cheapest: rain. Most large garden centers, home centers, and nurseries—especially in warmer parts of the country—now stock rain barrels of one type or another. The rain barrel is simply connected to downspouts or rainwater chains. There are a range of available designs, many of which are attractive or at least basic enough to blend in with your yard and landscape.

If you get bit by the environmental bug and want to take this idea one step further, you can use an in-ground rainwater harvesting tank with a pump. The rain is routed to the tank via feeder spouts. The tanks, usually made of stainless steel, store it for use later. When you're ready to water the lawn, you turn on the pump and connect your irrigation to the water outlet. It may seem like a rather drastic solution, but in areas where water bills skyrocket during warm months, and where local water resources are as much an environmental issue as an economic one, an in-ground rainwater runoff system can actually pay for itself over time.

Thinking Green: Gray Water ▸

Gray water is a hidden resource in every household that many homeowners are tapping in the face of increasing water shortages and rising water costs. Grey water is water reclaimed from clothes washers, bathtubs, showers, and sink drains throughout the house. Gray-water systems range from the incredibly simple to the complex. At the most basic, a gray-water system can be a sealed cistern fed by the clothes-washer discharge hose, with a drain hose attached. More complicated systems involve whole-house collection units with some type of filtering, and spigots for using the gray water outside.

Regardless of how basic or complex the system is, you need to check with your local authorities before ever installing one. Some municipalities outlaw the systems outright.

Tip ▸

As an emergency measure, you can use pool water to water your lawn. As long as you haven't chlorinated the pool within the previous four days, your lawn should be fine, and you can easily refill the pool when wetter weather returns.

Rain Barrels ▸

One of the simplest, most inexpensive, and most environmentally responsible ways to water a lawn is by tapping a system that collects rainwater and stores it for controlled irrigation. Although you should always check the acidity of your rainwater to ensure it is not too far out of balance, this source can account for a significant amount of water required by a thirsty lawn. The most common rain-barrel system includes one or more 40- or 80-gallon barrels connected to gutter downspouts. Spigots near the base of the barrels let you connect them to a hose. The barrels are usually plastic or stainless steel, although you can use a wooden cask if you prefer.

Some communities now offer subsidies for rain barrel systems, including free or low cost barrels and downspout connection kits. Check with your local water company or environmental protection agency.

Lawn Water Quality

Not all water is created equal. Depending on the source, the water you use on your lawn can bring with it a wide range of minerals, chemicals, and acidity. Well water, for instance, may be subject to infiltration from many sources such as fertilizer runoff from local farms, golf courses, or parks. Well water is also affected by the depth to which you had to drill to find water. Excess amounts of sulfur, salts, or minerals such as copper are not unheard of in well water.

Municipal water isn't necessarily pristine either. Although municipal water is treated at the source, any number of elements can be introduced along the way to your tap or spigot. Pipes carrying the water can contain high amounts of lead and copper. The city or locality may have introduced excessive amounts of chlorine if the authorities found high levels of bacteria or other organisms in water tests.

Obviously, you can't assume what comes out of your spigot and onto the lawn is necessarily the best water for your grass.

But even though serious imbalances tend to be rare and sporadic, simpler changes in the water can spell problems for your lawn. Hard water is the perfect example. Hard water—water containing high levels of calcium and magnesium—is usually good for the lawn. However, both city systems and in-home water softening systems introduce sodium to make the water "soft." If the level of sodium is high enough, it can turn grass leaves yellow and even do damage to the soil and the grass plants.

That's why whenever mysterious problems occur in a well-fed, well-tended lawn, it's wise to take a look at the water. If you have concerns, test the water. But at the very least, talk to the local cooperative extension office professional to find out if there have been issues with well or city water in your area.

Well water can contain minerals or have a level of acidity that can alter the makeup of your lawn's soil.

Water Testing ▶

Whenever you have concerns about your water, you'll only be engaging in educated guessing until you actually test the water or have it tested. As with soil, you can test your water with a home test kit, or choose the more expensive and more exacting option of a send-away lab test. Home tests are simple and quick to use. You just dip test strips into the sample and read the results. Most of these tests give you results measuring levels of chlorine, iron, copper, nitrates and nitrites, magnesium, and pH. Some also test for lead and pesticides.

Laboratory tests will give you more precise measurements of those contaminants, as well as levels of heavy metals, herbicides, specific fertilizers, and bacteria. Most water authorities offer testing services. Well water should usually be tested every year as a matter of course.

Lawn Watering Technology

When it comes to watering your lawn, it pays to use all the tools available. More effective lawn watering translates into a healthier lawn, a lower water bill, and an improved environment. Given the great importance of the issue in both a local and global sense, it should come as no surprise that it has spurred a wealth of scientific research and innovation. One of the most promising developments is evapotranspiration, known as ET.

ET is represented by a formula that calculates total water lost from soil evaporation and from the transpiration of the leaves of grass. The goal is to determine when and exactly how much water a lawn needs at any given moment. The ET formula is currently used in high-end automated sprinkler system controllers, in one of two ways. One type of controller uses a mounted weather gauge to gather local weather data, combining this with data about your specific yard, including the size of the lawn, type of grass, exposure, topography of the lawn surface, and other relevant features. The other type of controller gathers information by downloading it from weather satellites and other sources, including the Internet, combining that data with the particulars of your yard.

Both types then adjust sprinkler times to account for weather variations. It's an incredibly sophisticated approach to watering your lawn, but one that makes a lot of sense given how important water is almost everywhere today.

ET automated controllers and systems are not cheap. They add hundreds to the cost of a standard in-ground sprinkler system.

But ultimately, they can lower your water bill, make your lawn maintenance more environmentally friendly, and even lead to a healthier lawn. In the long run, they represent a pretty fair return on investment.

Rain sensors detect when a prescribed amount of rain has fallen and can be programmed to shut your automatic sprinkler system off, avoiding redundant watering. Other electronic systems pick up broadcasting weather forecasting information and adjust to the automated system that takes the weather into account.

Thinking Green: Wetting Agents ▸

Water can have a hard time getting to the roots of some lawns. The soil may become baked to a hard surface that repels water, so that the water evaporates before it is absorbed. Or your soil may have a high clay content and may be too dense to rapidly absorb moisture. The same goes for compacted soil. The results may be runoff or pooling that don't help the thirsty grass roots at all.

To remedy this situation, turn to wetting agents. Available in both liquid and granular forms, these compounds break the surface tension of the water, stopping it from beading and making it more easily absorbed.

Wetting agents, also known as surfactants, aren't meant for long-term use, and they don't add nutrients or actually improve the soil structure in any way. The best types are organic—granular types sometimes use cork as the carrier for the actual wetting agent. But be sure to check the label of any wetting agent you're considering because some contain ingredients that are not environmentally friendly. Lastly, avoid the old home remedy of using diluted dishwashing liquid—it can do more harm than good to grass plants.

Lawn Sprinklers

Water table and rainfall are not likely to be able to supply all the water your lawn needs to grow vigorously—not even close. That means you have to supplement nature's bounty to truly slake your lawn's thirst by watering in a way that dispenses the moisture efficiently. That's where sprinklers come in.

Many types of sprinklers are made and sold today, but they can be broken down into two categories: portable and in-ground systems. Portable sprinklers can be subdivided into four groups, defined by their method of dispersing water: rotary, oscillating, stationary, and spinning.

Installing an in-ground system is a major undertaking and a significant expense (see page 148). For an easier and cheaper option, turn to a portable sprinkler. But be aware that portable sprinklers are called "portable" because they need to be moved to get water everywhere it needs to go on the lawn. If you don't monitor it closely, the sprinkler can overwater some areas while leaving others almost dry.

When choosing a lawn sprinkler, the first factor you should consider is coverage. Some types work best in small areas, while others are superior at watering

An oscillating sprinkler is a good choice for both small and large lawns because you can control the coverage efficiently by varying the water pressure.

larger spaces. Smaller sprinklers are designed for control. This is handy if your lawn is an unusual shape with lots of corners and nooks, or if some areas are shaded or have other special considerations that affect the amount of water they need. However, using a sprinkler with a tight coverage pattern takes much more time and attention. If the whole lawn is roughly accessible from one point, it's wise to use a large-coverage sprinkler such as an oscillating unit or rotary sprinkler.

Even the best portable sprinkler will not cover a larger area uniformly. You need to know the pattern your sprinkler makes and compensate accordingly. The best way to check the coverage of your particular sprinkler is to perform the test described below.

Cost shouldn't be much of an issue in shopping for a portable sprinkler, because—with the exception of some models that are essentially yard art–they are all relatively inexpensive. Beware that some sprinklers have very uneven distribution. What you do want to look at when considering different sprinklers is their spray pattern and how that matches the shape, size, and configuration of your lawn. Give it some thought because a sprinkler that is poorly suited to your lawn will be an irritation that wastes water.

Thinking Green: Hose-End Timers ▶

The challenge with portable sprinklers is to run them just long enough to supply the water necessary for that area of the lawn. But once you get it going, it's easy to let your attention wander, or just forget the sprinkler is running. To prevent wasting water and ensure that your lawn doesn't become waterlogged, use a hose-end timer, placed between the spigot and the hose-end. Set the timer for the appropriate watering time, and enjoy the rest of your afternoon.

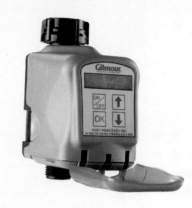

The Can Test ▶

To determine the rate at which your sprinkler dispenses water to different areas, clean out 8 to 10 tuna cans (or cat food cans, whichever is available) and place them in a random pattern around the sprinkler. Turn on the sprinkler and let it run for 15 minutes. Turn off the sprinkler and measure how much water is in the cans. That number times 4 is the hourly rate of your sprinkler, for each different area. If your goal is to spread ½" of water in two weekly waterings, determine how long you need to run the sprinkler by dividing .5 by the hourly rate. Supplement the areas that are underwatered as necessary.

Choosing a Sprinkler

If you're like many homeowners, the sprinkler you purchased was directed mostly by which model was on the shelf right in front of you. In fact, you should consider carefully when choosing a sprinkler (or multiple sprinklers) for your lawn. Each has its own strengths and weaknesses, and buying the wrong type can mean the difference between getting your lawn the water it needs, or wasting water on areas such as driveways, sidewalks, and gravel beds. Following is a sampling of the main lawn sprinkler types.

HOSE SPRAYER/HAND WATERING

The most basic type of lawn watering you can do is with an unadorned hose, capped by a spray nozzle that you aim to direct the water. You can buy fancy sprayers with multiple settings but that doesn't change the fact that it's extremely difficult to achieve even coverage across the surface of your lawn when watering by hand. And the time it would take is prohibitive. To distribute ½ inch of water by hand over a small lawn could easily take an hour or more. Hand watering is usually best reserved for very small patches of grass, or problem areas that can't be reached with sprinklers.

STATIONARY

These are the simplest sprinklers, with no moving parts to go wrong. The lack of moving parts, however, translates to very modest coverage. There are many different designs of stationary sprinklers, all with different spray patterns. All are extremely inexpensive.

The holes can sometimes get clogged, but the major drawback of this type of sprinkler is limited coverage area. Consequently, they only make sense for very small lawns. If you do choose a stationary sprinkler, be sure to buy one with a spray pattern that matches the shape of the small space you need to water.

SPINNING

The simplest versions of spinning sprinklers have three arms with spray holes. The arms are mounted on a swivel that sits atop a base. Water pressure causes the arms to spin, spraying the water in an arcing circle. Although spinning sprinklers are best on small lawns, the more expensive models have heavier bases and a wide spray radius, while cheaper models are lighter and have a tendency to flip over when used with maximum water pressure. Because the water from a spinning sprinkler falls in a circle around the base, you need to move the sprinkler periodically to create overlapping circles. Unless you happen to have a circular lawn, this design will waste water and overwater the overlap areas.

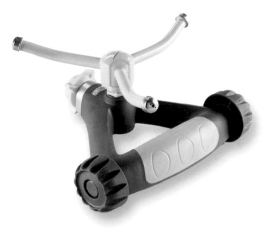

OSCILLATING

One the most popular portable sprinklers, oscillating sprinklers feature a single bowed arm lined with spray holes. Water pressure causes the arm to move back and forth, so that the spray waters a path, backward and forward. The best models have little or no hesitation at each end of the stroke, otherwise water saturates the lawn at that point. This type of sprinkler is also prone to water loss in gusty wind, so it's best to use it only on calm days. Because of the constantly moving arm, this type of sprinkler is also the one most prone to malfunction.

ROTARY

Featuring a sturdy base, rotary sprinklers have a vertical head that contains a water-pressure-powered gear mechanism that repeatedly shoots out a strong stream of water spray, moving side to side in the process. An impulse sprinkler is roughly the same design, but with a counterweight that rebounds each time the stream hits it, cutting off the stream in a jerkier motion. Either type is very effective across large areas of lawn, and the concentrated stream loses very little water to evaporation or wind gusts. This is the choice of many professionals who don't have an in-ground system to work with.

TRAVELING

Perhaps a good idea, but not quite fully achieved, the traveling sprinkler has wheels that slowly propel the unit back along the hose. It follows the layout of the hose you determine, but water distribution is unpredictable and not efficient over any substantial square footage. Today's versions are more oddities than practical watering options.

In-Ground Sprinkler Systems

Properly set up and monitored, an in-ground sprinkler system will waste less water and keep your lawn healthier than any other watering option. The key, of course, lies in that phrase "Properly set up and monitored."

All in-ground systems contain the same basic components and they are arranged in roughly the same layout. The system is fed by a connection to the home's main cold water supply line, which is routed through a vacuum breaker or backflow valve that prevents sprinkler system water from backing up into the home's supply.

The system's water supply is routed out to control valves that serve different zones. Each zone contains one or more sprinkler heads. The zone valves, supply pipes, and heads are all usually PVC, which is easy to work with and resists damage from movement during the freeze-thaw cycle.

The zone valves are controlled by a central controller. In the past, this was an analog unit wired with electricity that made use of a day-and-hour timer. The homeowner usually set it according to when he wanted the lawn to be watered.

Today's controllers are mostly digital models with much more programming flexibility built in. The problem is, most homeowners don't look to take advantage of the programming capabilities. Most people just set up their controller to trigger the sprinklers every day or every other day, at a certain time (usually early in the morning). Unfortunately, that doesn't take into account weather,

or a sudden drop or hike in temperature that will affect how much water the lawn requires.

Increasingly, homeowners are using more sophisticated controllers that calculate data from weather and soil sensors to determine if watering is actually necessary and, if so, how much water is appropriate. The high-end sprinkler system controllers offered today make use of the latest ET (envirotranspiration, see page 143) data and technology to water exactly when and how much your lawn needs. The only other way to get this kind of control, and to protect against water waste, is to control the system manually. Unfortunately, most homeowners probably chose an in-ground system precisely because they wanted to "set it and forget it," so monitoring it and adjusting it manually may well be disregarded. If you have made the decision to upgrade your lawn to an in-ground system, spend the extra money for a modern controller that will make more informed decisions, saving you water-bill money in the long run.

An in-ground sprinkler system can be the perfect watering solution, especially if you use a modern, data-driven controller.

Saving Sewer Fees ▶

Most municipalities charge a sewer fee based on your water meter, assuming that all the water that comes in goes out through a drain. This doesn't take into account the water used for irrigation, the biggest amount of which goes toward keeping your lawn healthy. Depending on your local rules and regulations, you may be able to save a handy sum on your sewer bill by installing what is known as a "submeter." This is basically a separate water meter logging the water routed to irrigation and outside uses such as watering the garden. The submeter reading is subtracted from your sewer fees.

The Contractor Option ▶

In-ground sprinkler systems require extensive excavation and plumbing. Installing one is a project that should be attempted only by experienced do-it-youselfers. If you aren't completely sure that your abilities, knowledge, and experience properly equip you for tackling this particular project, hire a contractor instead. Use only a licensed contractor who can provide you with proof of insurance. You don't want to find out the limits of your homeowner coverage if and when a worker is injured digging a trench for a sprinkler line. You should also check references to see if the contractor has successfully completed a project on par with yours, including the same or greater number of zones, and a similar controller installation. Make sure the contractor will warranty the equipment, whether he is selling it to you as part of the project, or you are getting it from a third party vendor. Ultimately, you want to be secure in the knowledge that if something goes wrong with any part of the system, quick help will be only a phone call away. As always, get everything in writing, including start and finish dates and warranty specifications (if the contractor is not supplying the materials, you'll want him to conform to all the manufacturer's requirements for maintaining the warranty).

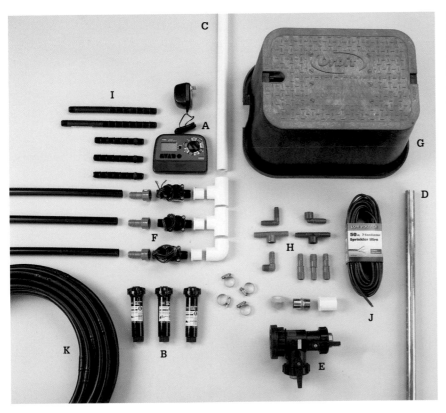

Parts of an inground sprinkler system include: Controller (A), sprinkler heads (B), PVC pipe (C), copper pipe (D), backflow preventer/vacuum assembly (E), control valve (F), control valve box (G), tees (H), funny pipe (I), low-voltage wire (J), polyethylene pipe (K).

How to Install an In-Ground Sprinkler System

Measure the flow rate of your water supply by setting a gallon bucket under an outdoor spigot. Open the faucet all the way and time how long it takes to fill the bucket. Calculate the system gallons per minute (GPM) by dividing 60 by the fill time. The GPM figure is needed to choose properly sized feeder pipe.

Measure the water pressure of your water supply system. Make sure all faucets in the house are off, and then attach a pressure valve to an exterior sillcock. Open the valve all the way and record the reading.

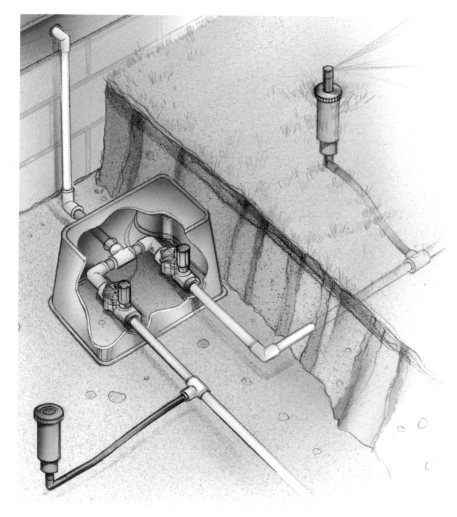

The fundamentals of an in-ground sprinkler system are shown here. The water-supply line draws water from the house's cold water supply, routing it to zone valves contained in an underground box. The water is then piped out to the sprinkler heads for each zone.

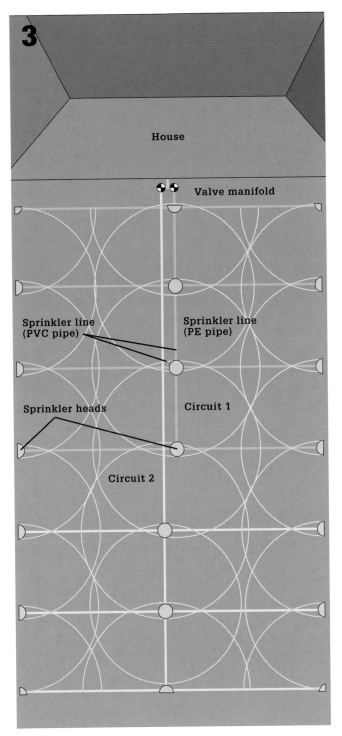

3

House

Valve manifold

Sprinkler line
(PVC pipe)

Sprinkler line
(PE pipe)

Sprinkler heads

Circuit 1

Circuit 2

4

Plan your system. Take measurements and sketch a rough layout of the lawn and yard with exact dimensions. Send this information, along with the pressure and GPM figures, to the manufacturer or third-party sprinkler plan creation company. Collect all the pieces for your system and check them against the plan. Check that you have the right number of each type of sprinkler head, and a sufficient amount of pipe and tubing.

Splice a tee fitting into the cold water supply line in the run just after the meter, inside or under the house. You may use copper or plastic supply pipe. If you choose plastic, you'll need to use a tee with compression-fittings and a copper-to-PVC adapter. You'll also need to connect a full-flow ball valve and vacuum breaker/back flow preventer. Some municipalities require this be done by a licensed contractor or plumber. Local codes may also require the vacuum assembly be connected inside. Drill a hole through the rim joist or foundation wall and run the supply pipe and controller wire out through the hole.

(continued)

Remove sod over the trenches and dig the trenches for sprinkler lines 8" to 10" deep. Do the same for the holes for the zone valves. Keep the sod on plastic next to the trenches, and regularly moisten it as you work.

Run the supply line and wire to the first control valve location. Line the bottom of the control-valve hole with gravel, and splice the valve body connections into the supply line.

Construct the zone-valve assembles and connect them to the supply-line. Install an in-line drain fitting, if required by code or as part of the system design, opposite the supply side of each valve.

Connect the control wires to the zone valves. Run supply lines to other zone valve locations, and finish them in the same way. Install the control-valve boxes and backfill around them. Make sure that the valves can be easily accessed through the box cover.

Run the main feed lines and branch lines from the control valves. Install drain valves at the lowest point in each feed line (or as required by local code), threaded into the valve with Teflon tape.

Create a hole for pipe to run under sidewalks by gluing a hose adapter to one end of a length of PVC pipe and a special tunneling nozzle (available at large home centers) to the other end. Spray from each side to create the pipe access hole.

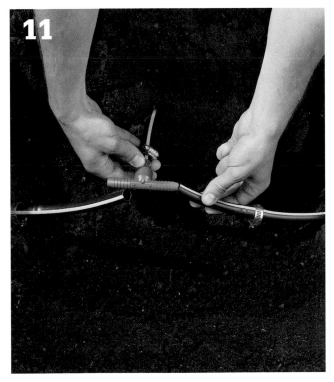

Cut polyethylene pipe with scissor cutters (use PVC pipe cutter on PVC pipe). Add tees for branch lines.

Install the sprinkler heads. In most cases, use a basic 90° fitting, although you may need to use a drain fitting at low points. Connect the head using funny pipe.

(continued)

13

If you've used a drain fitting, put gravel below it and over it when backfilling. Backfill the sprinkler head hole, being careful to keep the head level with the top surface. Tamp down the soil, leaving room for sod.

Alternative: When a sprinkler head is located directly over the supply pipe, use a tee connection with a threaded riser (you'll find them in a range of lengths).

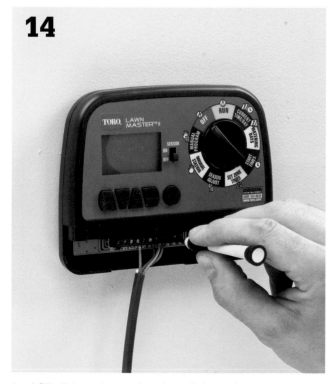

14

Backfill all trenches and replace all the sod you removed. Finally, wire in the control panel according to the manufacturer's wiring diagram and setup and test the system.

Rent a Pipe Puller ▶

If your yard is large and will require several long trenches for main and branch sprinkler lines, it may make sense for you to rent a pipe puller (sometimes called a vibratory plow). This machine uses a powerful blade on an arm that essentially burrows down to create a tunnel in which it runs the sprinkler pipe 12" to 16" below the surface of the soil. The machine is heavy to operate and fairly expensive to rent, but on a large project it will save many hours of time and hard labor. You'll still need to dig up the trench at junction points, such as wherever a head must be installed or for the zone control valves.

Adjusting In-ground Sprinklers

Modern in-ground sprinkler heads are extremely adjustable, something many homeowners don't realize because their contractors didn't tell them. You can adjust your sprinkler heads to account for variations in weather, wind, and anomalies in the lawn itself. However, in most cases, you'll only need to adjust the head right after the system is installed. Conditions affecting the need for water will usually be accounted for in your controller.

Rotary heads that spray a concentrated stream can be adjusted by twisting the collar on the body of the sprinkler. This allows you to direct the water exactly where you want it to go.

Spray heads can be adjusted to any of a number of spray patterns and angles using a special tool available from the manufacturer of the head.

The In-Ground System Alternative ▶

If you love the idea of an in-ground sprinkler system but can't quite manage the budget to install one, consider installing "hybrid" sprinkler heads instead. These are installed in the ground and look much like standard in-ground heads. The big difference is that these heads are connected to male and female hose adapters that allow you connect a garden hose to the head and, if you want, to connect another hose on the outflow side, to link several of the heads in series.

Winterizing the Lawn

Preparing the lawn to survive the winter months is almost as important as keeping it going strong during the growing season. Warm-season lawns in temperate parts of country continue to grow over the winter. *Note: Warm-season grasses should not receive "winterizer" or any other kind of fertilizer in the fall unless a cool-season grass is overseeded.*

The first step in winterizing a cool-season lawn is to apply a specially formulated fertilizer called *winterizer.* This is a formula high in potassium, which helps strengthen the cells of the grass plants and toughens them up for the winter to come. The potassium affects both top growth and roots, increasing the plant's ability to endure cold and helping it take up other essential nutrients prior to going dormant.

The last time you mow the grass at the end of the growing season, set the mower lower so that you cut to a grass height of around 2" or less. This will limit damage to the grass and prevent it from becoming a haven for rodents during the colder months. Water the lawn well one last time before the first freeze.

It's also very important that the lawn not be covered with leaves or other yard debris over the winter months. Any covering can damage the lawn, adding to the stress of colder temperatures. Remove leaves and give the lawn a brisk raking to clear all debris from between the grass plants. Once you're finished with that, make sure all your lawn-care equipment and tools are cleaned, serviced, and stored. Then head inside and keep yourself warm until spring, when your lawn will need you again.

Sprinkler System Hibernation ▶

If you live in an area where the ground freezes, you'll need to prepare your in-ground sprinkler system for winter. Turn the supply line off using the valve at the T between the cold water supply and sprinkler system supply. Then use the system's drain valve to completely drain the lines.

Removing the layer of fall leaves sitting on your lawn ensures that the grass plants don't develop disease over the winter months.

Using a Leaf Blower/Vacuum

A leaf blower can make quick work out of clearing the lawn of leaves, especially if your town has curbside pickup. The blowing action also clears organic debris down to the soil (inset), helping ready the lawn for winter.

Using a blower/vac to pick up leaves is a quick way to gather them for your own compost pile.

Disposing of Fall Leaves

If your municipality collects leaves at curbside, rake them onto a large tarp, such as a plastic painter's tarp, and drag them to the curb for pickup.

Some sanitation departments require that leaves be put in biodegradable bags for pickup. But even if they don't, it's the ecologically responsible thing to do.

THE LAWN PROBLEM-SOLVER GUIDE

Solving Lawn Problems

Your first line of defense against any invaders or flaws in the lawn is simple plant health. If you take care of the lawn with the right nutrition, the proper amount of hydration, and fastidious maintenance, you'll be giving it the best chance flourish.

Unfortunately, there is always the possibility that something is going to cause damage or try to overtake the real estate. In creating the perfect circumstances for a lawn to thrive, you're creating a very inviting habitat for all kinds of plants and insects (even the undesirable ones).

Not to worry. There are solutions for every malady a lawn may suffer. Of course, you need to know what to look for. That's why this chapter includes photo guides of the lawn's most common foes, along with appropriate treatments you need to beat them and keep your grass in the peak of health.

In this chapter:

- Fighting Weeds
- Defeating Harmful Insects & Pests
- Dealing With Lawn Diseases
- Improving Site Conditions
- Installing a French Drain
- Creating a Drainage Swale
- Adding a Mowing Strip
- Artificial Lawns

Fighting Weeds

We tend to think of weeds as the sworn enemies of the lawn, but in fact they are just different plants looking for a place of their own. Of course, that doesn't much matter, when they show up as blights on what is otherwise a pristine, uniform, deep green lawn.

That's when the gauntlet is thrown down, the gloves come off, and the weapons come out. But really, before you start fighting a weed or weeds, you need to understand what you're dealing with. If you're going to beat it, you need to know how and when it grows. That starts with the knowledge that not all weeds are created equal.

There are many ways to classify weeds. Like turfgrasses, there are warm-season and cool-season weeds. A warm-season weed flourishes in the heat of summer, while cool-season species actively grow in spring and fall. Either kind may be found in either season of lawn.

Another useful grouping in terms of heading off weeds before they grow is into annuals, biennials, and perennials.

Bluegrass

- **Annuals.** Like annual flowers, annual weeds live their entire life in one growing season. The classification is a little deceptive, however, because if an annual weed matures and produces seeds, new annual weeds will arrive next year. This means you can break the cycle by simply disrupting the creation, dissemination, or germination of those seeds. Common annuals include prostrate knotweed and annual bluegrass.
- **Biennials.** Biennials have a two-year lifecycle. They spend the first year using all their energy to grow, setting down strong roots and establishing themselves in the soil. The second year is focused on flowering and setting seed. These are tough plants to eradicate, because if you don't kill or remove the first-year root, they will come back with flowers and seeds in year two. Mallow is a common biennial and a familiar interloper in many lawns.

Crabgrass is a common lawn invader and one that is quick to spread in just about any area your turfgrass finds inhospitable. Once it has a foothold, it will gradually invade healthier parts of your lawn, too. Crabgrass is a warm-season annual. Apply a pre-emergent before hot weather and mow lawn high to smother.

Mallow

Creeping Charlie

- **Perennials.** Perennial weeds live for multiple years. They will continue through a cycle of dormancy and active growth, and may even fool you into thinking you've eradicated them. Some perennials spread through rhizomes and stolons, making them even more difficult to permanently remove from the lawn. The secret is to kill the whole plant, preferably before they flower and set seed. Dandelion and Creeping Charlie are two common perennials.

In addition to their growth periods, weeds are classified based on appearance: Broadleaf weeds have relatively wide leaves with branching veins. Many have conspicuous flowers. Narrow-leafed weeds have grass-like leaves with parallel veins. Dandelion and oxalis are two common broadleaf weeds, while Bermuda grass (in cool-season lawns) and crabgrass are examples of narrow-leaf weeds. The distinction is important because they respond to different herbicides.

Regardless of how you classify them, all weeds are opportunistic plants that look to take advantage of conditions turfgrass finds challenging. Some weeds will infiltrate a wet area at the first sign of boggy conditions. Others can thrive in hot, waterless conditions that leave most turfgrasses withered, brown, and sparse.

The problem is, even after those conditions have been remedied, the weed will staunchly hold onto the ground it has gained. That's one of the many reasons why it's so important to not let adverse conditions linger in the lawn. If weeds have made it in, you'll have to decide between turning to chemical remedies, or using more labor-intensive, but less toxic, natural cures. Whichever remedy you choose, keep in mind that a completely weed-free lawn is a very hard objective to achieve and, many would argue, not completely desirable. Some weeds bring beneficial diversity to the lawn and can even help maintain soil and lawn health.

Dandelion

Compact-Soil Weeds ▶

Weeds will take advantage of poor soil conditions. They are tough plants that can flourish in soil that would stymie most turfgrasses. That's why basic lawn hygiene and soil maintenance are so important. One poor soil condition that creates a prime breeding ground for weeds is compaction. Weeds such as crabgrass, plantain, and chickweed have no problem thriving in compacted soil and will move right in to push more desirable grasses aside. The best remedy for compacted soil is timely situational aeration (see page 54). It is also wise to eliminate controllable sources of the compaction, such as car or foot traffic.

Identifying Common Weeds

When it comes to weeds, it's wise to know the enemy—which means recognizing them on sight. The one big advantage any homeowner has over these lawn invaders is that most weeds stick out. The following listings are divided into the sneakier narrow-leaf species that often blend right in with the lawn while they spread throughout the turf, and the brazen broad-leaf types that announce themselves with distinctive appearances. Once you determine the specific weed you're dealing with, follow-up with the appropriate treatment.

Narrow-Leaf Weeds

CRABGRASS

Perhaps the best-known and most ubiquitous lawn weed, crabgrass, is sometimes also called Devil's grass—for good reason. This warm-season annual will sneak into a cool-season lawn during hot, dry weather. It spreads seeds that sprout in spring, but the thick branching stems can root at joints. In a compromised lawn, crabgrass will spread quickly, filling in bare spots.

Treatment: Crabgrass is relatively easy to pull, because the fibrous root bundle grows close to the surface. As prevention, apply a preemergence herbicide in late winter or early spring (crabgrass herbicides are often part of weed-and-feed combinations). Enrich the soil with compost and calcium. Dense, healthy lawns rarely allow crabgrass invasion. Mow high.

Crabgrass

ANNUAL BLUEGRASS

As the name says, this is a cool-season annual that is quick to sprout and spread as soon as warm weather hits in spring. You can tell it from Kentucky bluegrass by its lighter green color. It features small white seedheads, which give the lawn an overall whitish hue. Annual bluegrass loves moisture and it will pop

Annual bluegrass

up in boggy conditions or where water puddles on top of poorly draining soil. It can't take heat, and will often yellow, wither, and die in the height of summer drought—but not before spreading seed that germinates through fall.

Treatment: Mow higher than normal if you know annual bluegrass will be a problem, and alleviate any drainage problems, especially low-lying areas that collect water, before the season starts. You can treat with a preemergence herbicide in fall just as the weather cools. Do not use herbicide if your fall maintenance will include overseeding.

QUACKGRASS

Similar in appearance to crabgrass but with thicker stems, quackgrass is a clump-forming perennial that will grow up to 3 ft. tall if left uncut. The bluish-green stems are hollow and end in wheatlike spikes. It spreads through rhizomes and can consequently be difficult to entirely eradicate.

Treatment: Quackgrass is a tough enemy, because a tiny piece of rhizome can grow into a brand-new plant. Don't attempt to pull the grass, because this may stimulate rhizome growth. Cut back new growth constantly in spring and carefully apply a non-selective herbicide to individual plants. The stronger you make your turfgrass, the more it will crowd out the quackgrass. But if your entire lawn is infested, you really have two choices: kill the lawn and start again, or live with the quackgrass.

Quackgrass

DALLIS GRASS

A clump-forming, warm-season perennial, dallis grass sends down deep roots that support long stems growing out of the crown in a star pattern. The leaves are coarse, and fingerlike segments sprout from the tips of the stems. This grass starts growing in early spring and is a common enemy of warm-season grasses. It thrives in moist, hot areas. It grows best in lawns that have been allowed to grow high. Dallis grass reproduces by seeds and rhizomes and can grow from segments of rhizomes left over after tilling or pulling the weed. It sprouts in spring and thrives throughout summer.

Treatment: Don't bother trying to pull the weed; it will just come back. Use a postemergence herbicide such as glysophate to spot-treat outbreaks of individual plants, and repeat once a week for three weeks to ensure the plant is eradicated. Head off the establishment of dallis grass in your turf by mowing regularly.

Dallis grass

Barnyard grass

BARNYARD GRASS

A tough survivor, this grass grows in poor soil and neglected and sparse areas of the lawn. It is a shallow-rooted summer annual that usually grows tall and erect, but will form mats if regularly mowed. It reproduces by seed, and grows signature purple seedheads on thick, reddish purple stems.

Treatment: The best defense is a highly fertile soil and dense turf. Individual weeds can be pulled or, in the case of extensive mats, spot-treated with a nonselective herbicide. You may have to reapply it two or three times over the course of one or two weeks, until the weed is completely dead. Use a preemergence herbicide in early spring, just as the weather warms.

Sedges ▸

Sedges are a group of perennials and annuals that resemble common, cool-season grasses. Even in a conscientiously mowed and maintained lawn, sedges may go unnoticed. The most distinctive features of most sedge species are their seedheads. Two common lawn invaders, purple nutsedge and yellow nutsedge, are named for the color of their seedheads. The leaves are very similar to grass leaves, although if you roll a sedge stem between your fingers, you'll notice that the stems are actually triangular, as opposed to the round stems of most turfgrasses. In addition, sedges have three leaves per stem, while turfgrasses generally have two.

Sedges are prolific plants that reproduce by seeds, rhizomes, and tubers. Pulling sedges doesn't have much effect. It may seem like you have removed all the plant, while it has actually left tubers behind to sprout the following year. These weeds prefer wet or even boggy conditions, in otherwise nutrient-rich soils.

Treating sedges requires persistence and painstaking lawn maintenance. Start by making sure that you are conservative in your lawn watering, and that every part of the lawn drains well. The best direct treatment is a selective "nutsedge" herbicide applied in early spring, and reapplied several times over the following two weeks. Repeat at the same time the following year, to ensure the weeds don't reappear.

WITCH GRASS

A summer annual that grows upright with a tasseled flowerhead and fleshy, shallow roots, witch grass reproduces by seed. The foliage is hairy and the seedheads are grayish brown, and spread the seed when they break off from the stem. The stems can also root at nodes. Witch grass grows best in compacted conditions along driveways, walkways and curbs, and rarely takes hold in well-maintained lawns.

Treatment: It is easy to pull, but important that it be pulled at first sign of growth, long before seedheads have a chance to drop and spread seed. It can also be mowed to prevent seedheads from growing. Apply a preemergence herbicide in early spring, right after the weather warms.

Witch grass

Foxtail

FOXTAIL

This summer annual is common in lawns bordering wild fields and rural areas, from which it will migrate. It's easily detected by the characteristic seedhead that looks like its namesake. It is a nuisance for dogs, often breaking off and sticking deep in their ears. It thrives in the heat of summer and suffers under repeated mowing, which can kill the plant. Foxtail prefers rich, well-drained soil.

Treatment: Foxtails are easy to pull and can be mowed down, although if seedheads are mowed, the clippings should be bagged and disposed of. Foxtail can be controlled or prevented with a preemergence herbicide in early spring.

Moss Madness ▶

Moss can't really be considered a weed, because it's more a symptom than a problem itself. If moss is growing it's because several undesirable conditions exist in that area of the lawn. The most prevalent will be excess moisture, because moss dries out and dies very quickly in a dry, well-drained environment. Its presence also indicates infertile soil that is in need of nutrients. It also thrives in shallow soil and deep shade.

Although you can find both synthetic and organic moss-killing products (such as herbicidal soap) on the market, the real issue and the ultimate solution is to clear up the underlying causes that sparked the moss to flourish in the first place.

Goose grass

GOOSE GRASS

This clump-forming annual can look a little like crabgrass when it is cut low, and it will spread into mats. The seedheads grow like spikes at the end of stems, and the stems are prone to collapsing and laying flat on the ground. It grows widespread roots, making it difficult to remove by pulling. Goose grass likes compacted, poor quality soil.

Treatment: Eradicate clumps of goose grass by spot-treating with a non-selective herbicide, waiting about a week before digging out the plant (the herbicide should kill the weed's roots, but top growth may still appear alive). You can use a preemergence herbicide in late spring, but loose soil and dense turf will prevent goose grass infiltration.

NIMBLEWILL

This warm-season perennial features wiry, spreading growth, with flat, bluish-green leaves. The appearance mimics many turfgrasses, but if allowed to grow, it will produce feather-like seedheads in fall. Nimblewill spreads through both seeds and stolons.

Nimblewill

Treatment: Nimblewill is easy to pull, and this is the preferred method of eradication. It thrives under the same conditions most turfgrasses prefer, so changing lawn conditions will not affect the growth of nimblewill. If infestation is widespread, use a selective herbicide labeled for use on nimblewill, from late spring through the beginning of summer. Keep the lawn mowed to the correct height to prevent the formation of seedheads in fall.

WILD ONION AND WILD GARLIC

Welcome in the herb garden, these species are considered hostile invaders in a lawn. Both grow from bulbs and reproduce from seeds or bulblets, making them somewhat different from other weeds. Wild onions will grow bulbs or seeds on the tip of the tall stems if allowed to grow high—their means of reproducing. Both plants have fleshy, tubular leaves. They are dormant over winter and spread in spring and summer. But the most obvious characteristic of both these plants is the odor. Wild onion smells strongly of onion, while wild garlic smells just as strongly of garlic.

Treatment: These plants are easy to pull or, if it is your preference, to harvest. Just make sure you dig up all bulbs and bulblets when weeding. Regular mowing helps keep both wild onion and wild garlic controlled and stops them from spreading. In the event of infestation, use a selective herbicide in spring, repeating applications as necessary into the summer. Ultimately, to get rid of any traces of these two plants, you'll need to use the herbicide for two to three years.

Wild garlic

Broadleaf Weeds

BROADLEAF PLANTAIN

One of the most common weeds, this perennial intruder grows light green leaves in a rosette pattern. It grows slender, tall seed stalks in fall, and the plant is deeply rooted with strong fleshy roots and a stubborn central taproot. Like many other weeds, broadleaf plantain thrives in constantly moist, compacted soil.

Treatment: Although pulling the complete plant is work and not always successful (this works best if you catch them young, long before the seedheads develop), broadleaf plantain is easy to eradicate with selective post-emergence broadleaf herbicides.

Dandelion

Broadleaf plantain

DANDELION

There's no mistaking this flashy lawn invader. The bright yellow flowers are markers of spring in fields everywhere, and in lawns across the country. The flowers are followed closely by puffy snowball seedheads that explode and send seeds scattering to the wind. The serrated leaves grow out from a central crown, which is fed by a deep, tight-holding root.

Treatment: Dandelions are relatively easy to treat with a selective preemergence herbicide applied in fall. One application should be plenty to kill the entire plant. You can also use this same treatment in early spring. In the course of the season, use non-selective broadleaf herbicides for spot treatments; pulling the plants is effective if you remove all or most of the root. *Note: Research indicated that dandelions wear out and die if you keep after them, although there is some re-growth from incompletely removed roots.*

CURLY DOCK

Reddish leaves with wavy margins define this perennial, and make it look a little like a dandelion that is not in bloom. It spreads by seeds that are grown on a tall, thin, green seedheads, but is fairly easy to contain and eradicate.

Curly dock

Thinking Green: Dandy-Lions ▶

If you're willing to put up with the appearance of a few dandelions in the lawn, you can realize some benefit from them. Dandelion greens are edible and can be added to salads (wash them very well first). They are also a favorite treat for domesticated rodents, such as guinea pigs. In your soil, the root growth creates gaps for earthworms and other beneficial organisms, and the flowers are an early food source for honeybees.

Chickweed

Treatment: Curly dock is one of the less resistant weeds, and can usually be eradicated with a single application of a general broadleaf herbicide. Individual plants can be dug out as long as all of the plant is removed. Mowing regularly to standard heights usually keeps the plant from spreading seed.

CHICKWEED

A common, mat-forming annual, chickweed does not usually infiltrate healthy, dense lawns. Instead, it tends to grow into bare patches or areas that would not support vigorous grass growth. These include heavily shaded and moist corners of the yard, and gravel pathways. It grows yellow-green leaves along spreading stems with small white flowers in spring. The stems can root at nodes. The seeds germinate in early fall.

Treatment: Chickweed is a very easy weed to pull, and extracting the entire plant is simple and practically effortless. To prevent recurrence, you should improve the soil or conditions in the area the weed covered, and if the problem is severe, you can treat with a general post-emergence broadleaf herbicide, or proactively, with a pre-emergence product in early fall, just as the weather cools.

ENGLISH DAISY

A favorite perennial in the flower garden, this flowering plant will quickly invade the lawn if given a chance. The pretty white flowers with yellow centers grow over softly lobed leaves, starting in spring and sometimes in fall. It does best in lawn soil that is deficient in nutrients and consistently wet. Growth of the tall stems is fueled by a deep taproot, and the plant spreads through seeds. Before you rid your lawn of this plant, cut the flowers for indoor displays and, if you're so inclined, make tinctures or teas from the greens.

English daisy

Treatment: You can pull English daisy plants by hand, but you need to be sure to get the whole plant, including all of the taproot. Fertilize to increase the nutrient density in the soil, and if you suspect they will be a problem, use a general weed-and-feed product that includes a selective broadleaf herbicide.

SPEEDWELL

In the right place and circumstance, speedwell is considered a groundcover for its habit of spreading far and wide in a tight-knit mat. It's actually a wildflower, with stems filled with pretty purple blossoms over tiny, hairy green round leaves. However, in a lawn, it's one of the first weeds to appear, usually right at the end of winter. Speedwell loves cool, wet conditions and thrives in shade. It's a vigorous opponent to homeowners looking for a pristine lawn, and in addition to spreading seed, mowing can spread the plant. Small sections will root and grow independently.

Treatment: The first line of defense against speedwell is to make sure every part of the lawn is well drained, and that any shady areas are opened up by cutting back trees and shrubs to allow plentiful sunlight over the lawn. Hand pulling is effective and easy, but you really have to be sure you get the whole plant, because one small piece can grow anew. If you decide to attack with chemicals, you'll need to use a selective broadleaf herbicide, and probably more than one application will be necessary to completely eradicate the speedwell.

Speedwell

HENBIT

Henbit is a winter annual, following an unusual cycle of growth. It features sprawling square stems with somewhat fuzzy, round, scalloped leaves. Henbit grows from seed, sprouting in fall, and then growing throughout winter, only to bloom in mid spring, after which it dies. It's important to know this cycle if you're going to eradicate the plant.

Treatment: It's fairly easy to pull henbit by hand, but if the weed seems out of control in your lawn, you can use weed-and-feed post-emergence application using a product labeled for henbit. You can also apply pre-emergence herbicide in early fall to kill seeds.

Prostrate knotweed

Henbit

PROSTRATE KNOTWEED

Yet another annoying mat-forming weed, prostrate knotweed is a summer annual that starts growing as soon as the soil warms. Like many other weeds, it thrives in poor soil and in problem areas such as high-traffic driveway edges, along shortcut paths across the lawn, and in similar locations in which soil is compacted. The plant sends out wiry stems with smooth, oval, blue green leaves. It also produces a tough taproot. Prostrate knotweed reproduces from seed.

Clover: Friend or Foe? ▶

Many organic gardeners would contend that far from being an invader that needs to be fought or eradicated, clover should be embraced as an ally in the war against other weeds and nutrient deficiencies.

Traditional white clover, with its small pretty flowers and signature simple round leaves in groups of three or—if you're lucky—four, can be a boon to lawn health. Clover is infected by rhizobia, a soil bacteria that spurs the plant to create nodules on roots that "fix" or hold nitrogen. This allows clover to convert nitrogen in the air for use in the plant. Mowing and mulching clover in the lawn helps feed the lawn with slow-release nitrogen (and it also smells fantastic). If the lawn contains 5 to 10 percent clover, the clover can supply almost all the yearly nitrogen needs of the turfgrass. Clover also remains green all year round, and can help make the lawn more resistant to disease.

The look certainly isn't for everyone, and certainly not for the homeowner trying to create an immaculate lawn. But if you can put up with a few round leaves amongst your blades of grass, you'll enjoy a bounty of organic benefits.

Treatment: In spite of the taproot, it's not difficult to pull individual prostrate knotweed plants. You do, however, have to make sure to get all the root and crown to eliminate the plant. Treat infestations in early spring, with a selective broadleaf post-emergence herbicide. Here again, improving the low-quality conditions that allow the plant to flourish will go a long way toward preventing its return.

GROUND IVY (CREEPING CHARLIE)

A highly aggressive perennial, ground ivy can be a serious threat to your lawn. The plant features various-sized round leaves with scalloped edges. It spreads both by seed and by creeping stems that can root. It forms a dense mat that can quickly crowd out healthy lawns, and although it prefers poor quality soil and shade, it can thrive in sun and loam as well.

Treatment: If you notice ground ivy in nearby yards, chances are you're going to be dealing with it in yours eventually. Take quick and decisive action. Optimum lawn and soil health are essential, but in and of themselves, no guarantee of deterrence. Spot treat with a non-selective herbicide, and apply a selective broadleaf herbicide in fall. You can also use a weed-and-feed product labeled for use on ground ivy.

Ground ivy

MALLOW

Distinctive, dark green crinkled leaves set mallow apart from other weeds. It's also one of the more tenacious species, growing into a low mat, with pink flowers in the leaf joints throughout summer. It has a significant taproot and will spread wherever the soil is deficient in nitrogen and other nutrients, and high in potassium. It can be an annual or biennial, but either form is difficult to eradicate.

Mallow

Treatment: You can pull mallow, but once it's established, you'll usually need to be a bit more aggressive than hand-pulling each plant. Add nitrogen to the soil in the form of fertilizer or organic topdressing, and mow regularly to the proper height for the grass. Use a weed-and-feed product labeled for use on mallow, and spot treat with a non-selective herbicide.

GARLIC MUSTARD

It may sound delicious to some, but garlic mustard is an invasive, biennial herb that poses a significant ecological threat because it routinely outcompetes native plants. Its seeds can remain viable in the ground for five years, complicating its eradication. In its first year the plant exists as a low-to-the-ground rosette of leaves. In its second year it will grow stalks that can reach up to 3 feet in height if not mown.

Treatment: Thorough hand-pulling of the entire plant can be effective for light infestations, but be sure to remove the plant immediately. For larger infestations, cut any flowering stems within a few inches of the ground, and treat with a systemic glyphosate herbicide.

Garlic mustard

Fighting Weeds Naturally

The first and best weapon in your war on weeds should be a strong, dense, healthy lawn. Even if you manage to accomplish this, however, there are many aggressive species that just won't quit until they've infiltrated and attempted to take over the lawn. But before you go reaching for chemical herbicides, get busy pulling weeds. Although some weeds are so well rooted that pulling them can be fruitless, many weeds can be pulled easily and effectively. Narrow leaf weeds, for example, are best controlled with hand pulling. If they do come back, pull them again and you weaken the plant further until it no longer has the energy to start from scratch.

If weeding is not an option for you, there are a number of natural alternatives to spot treat weeds of all kinds. These include pouring salted boiling water over the weed, and spraying with vinegar or citrus-based solutions. You'll find organic spot weed-treatment sprays at home centers and garden stores, and some natural food stores.

A simple weed puller can make extracting even deep-rooted weeds such as these dandelions a fairly easy chore. The tool also helps ensure that you pull as much of the root system as possible so the plant is less likely to grow back.

Corn gluten is an all-natural herbicide that also contains beneficial nitrogen. It will prevent weed seeds from germinating but will not kill existing weeds. Proper application time is critical.

Perhaps the most lethal weapon in the natural lawn care armory is corn gluten. This by-product of corn processing is used as a pre-emergence treatment for weeds of all kinds. The gluten is spread with a spreader just like fertilizer or lawn seed. It must be laid down two to three weeks before seed germination for the weed you're attacking, however. Contact your local cooperative extension service office to find out weed germination dates in your area.

Corn gluten has certain benefits in addition to its herbicidal qualities. It is about 10% nitrogen, so an application can greatly reduce the amount of nitrogen rich fertilizer your lawn needs from other sources. Corn gluten breaks down slowly, so the nitrogen is released over time, and it's a completely environmentally safe option.

The drawbacks to corn gluten are its substantial price tag and the fact that you can't spread it within six weeks of overseeding a lawn or the new seeds won't germinate. It also won't affect existing annual, perennial, or biennial weeds.

Just the same, corn gluten is part of a group of natural solutions, all of which should be considered before you turn to the riskier use of chemical weed killers.

Thinking Green: Torching Weeds ▸

Some weeds can be eradicated by pulling and some can't. Another option is using a basic DIY torch, or a special "flamer" with a feed hose and a long wand. You can direct an intense, tiny flame exactly where you want it go. Then burn the weed to death. It lends a whole new meaning to the term "scorched earth."

The heat of the flame not only fries top growth, it causes the liquids in the entire plant—including the roots—to become superheated. In most cases, a single burning will destroy an annual weed outright. Perennial weeds, and those with deep, stubborn root systems may take more than one burning, but keep at it. They too will eventually die under the flame.

Safety, of course, is paramount when using a flamer.

- Use an igniter like the type used to light gas grills. Matches can result in nasty finger burns. Better yet, purchase a torch with electronic ignition.
- Don't use a torch near flammable yard waste and debris. This includes a dry layer of thatch, tanbark pathways, or in a lawn that has been parched by drought.
- Use the torch for only a second or two at a time, repeating as necessary to completely destroy the weed. Sustaining the flame too long can damage soil and adjacent grass.
- Handle the torch or flamer with care, making sure not to contact the hot tip with your skin, and storing the fuel tank out of reach of children.

A propane torch dispenses with just about any weed quickly. Look for a torch with a hose and wand-style head, and push-button ignition. Hooked up to a 20-pound propane tank, this type of torch is portable and doesn't require you to bend over or work on your knees.

Synthetic Weed Killers

The field of chemistry has done wonders in coming up with ways to fight any invasion of weeds in your lawn. You'll find an amazing diversity of herbicides—the name for any chemical designed to kill plant life—at nurseries, garden stores, and home centers. Many of these are even formulated to eradicate specific classes of weeds.

To use any herbicidal product correctly and responsibly, you need to determine if it's the right type of herbicide for the weeds you're attempting to eliminate, and for your lawn, yard, and garden. You'll choose between granular and liquid products, but beyond that, there are several other important distinctions.

Pre-emergence herbicides kill seeds as they germinate, before they have the chance to "emerge" as plants. They are most effective at permanently eradicating annual weeds, although they may work on some species of perennials that grow solely from seeds. They will be far less effective against weeds that spread through rhizomes or stolons.

Post-emergence herbicides are formulated to kill existing weeds. They are organized into two interrelated pairs of categories:

Contact herbicides kill any plant matter to which they are applied. This means top growth will be quickly killed. But that doesn't necessarily mean that the weed is gone—its roots may be able to produce another plant. Systemic herbicides infiltrate the entire plant and are more complete solutions. The entire plant is killed.

Selective formulas are created for one category, such as broad-leaf weeds, to destroy only those plants and leave other surrounding flora alive. *Non-selective formulas* kill plant life indiscriminately, and will take out turfgrasses as quickly as weeds. These are usually sold as spot-use sprays that can kill a single plant or group with a directed application.

In using any herbicide it's essential that you use it at the right stage of the growing season. You should also err on the side of caution, using less than you need, rather than more. You can always reapply an herbicide, but using too much can cause dangerous side effects and damage your lawn just as surely as it destroys weeds. Lastly, look for the least toxic forms you can buy; these include glyphosate and glufosinate-ammonium formulations.

Spot treatments of selective formulations are often the best use of chemical herbicides.

Pre-emergence herbicide

Post-emergence herbicide

Herbicidal Soap ▸

An alternative to more toxic compounds, herbicidal soap can be used as a broad-spectrum, non-selective herbicidal for spot treatments. The soap works by destroying plant cell walls where it contacts the plant, drying out and killing the tissue. Herbicidal soap works best on seedlings and moss, and may require several applications to effectively destroy weeds with deep taproots, or perennial weeds. The best part is that the soap breaks down completely in two days.

Warning ▸

Chemicals that are formulated to destroy plant life usually are harmful to humans and other animals as well. Herbicide formulations are regulated and meant to be safe for home use when used as directed and in a cautious, mindful manner. The Environmental Protection Agency classifies herbicides with Roman numeral ratings of I through IV, from the most toxic (I) to the least (IV). To be on the safe side, limit your use of chemical herbicides to those rated III or IV. But even with the safer formulations you must follow all safe-use practices and precautions:

- Follow to the letter the instructions on the bag or bottle of herbicide.

- If you're applying granular herbicide with a spreader, make sure that the spreader is properly calibrated.
- If you're spraying an herbicide, don't do it on a windy day.
- Keep pets and children off the lawn for 24 hours after applying herbicides.
- Wear a mask and gloves (whether the label says to or not).
- Take your shoes off before going into the house, after you've walked over an area treated with herbicides.
- Take steps to limit any runoff from watering after applying herbicides. You should prevent them from making their way into the storm drain system, waterways, or adjacent properties.

Defeating Harmful Insects & Pests

Perhaps the greatest challenge when dealing with insect invaders in your lawn is identifying if the problem you're having is actually caused by insects and, if so, which species. That is made all the harder because signs of insect damage can look like a lot of other problems, including drought, disease, and pet damage. Added to that is the fact that insects have very rapid life cycles. They change quickly, well within the course of a lawn's growing season. That means that there is usually a period when the pests are most vulnerable, creating a window for eradication. Treating for insect infestation at the wrong time is just as inefficient as using the wrong treatment. The stages of a typical insect lifecycle include hatching from an egg, from which they go into the larval stage (the stage where the most damage is often caused), pupation in a cocoon-like phase, and emergence as adult winged insects.

Other insects, such as chinch bugs, go through a different development cycle. They become nymphs after hatching from eggs, essentially becoming small adults without wings. As they mature, their wings grow and they take flight. If you try to fight the insects at this point, you'll have little success.

Another difference separating insect species is the way in which they attack the lawn. Some go for the roots, while others will eat top growth. Still others act like vampires, sucking the juice out of grass blades and leaving toxins behind. However they operate, all insects are attracted by a healthy, dense, fast-growing lawn. It's a feast waiting to be plundered.

Finding insects is a matter of looking for them where and when they are active. If you've detected damage that you think is insect related, you need to actually see the insects to confirm your diagnosis. Dig under the sod and check the soil. Cutworms, for instance, eat the roots, so that the sod will come up too easily and you'll see the actual worms. Inspect the area at night as well, because some insects are only active after dark. If possible, capture one or more of the insects and either use the photo identifications in the pages that follow, or take it to a local cooperative extension office or nursery to have the insect identified. The experts who can identify the insect will more than likely be able to instruct you on appropriate eradication methods.

If the damage happens during one part of the year, every year, chances are you have an insect that is moving on after it matures. In that case, you want to mark the calendar and treat the pest in the larval stage to prevent recurrence. Visually identify the insect before you attempt to fight it.

Testing for Insects ▸

There is no room for guesswork when you're determining what treatment to use for an insect problem. To confirm which pest you have, turn to some simple tests. Discover chinch bugs by cutting the bottom out of a coffee can or similar can, sinking it into the lawn several inches, and filling the aboveground portion with water. Keep filling to maintain the level of water in the can and, if you have chinch bugs, they'll float to the top within about five minutes. You can also detect mole crickets and sod webworms this way.

Another more generalized test is to mix a couple of tablespoons of lemon dishwashing soap in a gallon of water. Slowly pour the mixture over a section of lawn about a yard square. Within about 8 to 10 minutes, any mole crickets, billbugs, cutworms, and sod webworms will come right to the surface, driven out by the soap.

Whatever damage you find, and whatever insect is causing it, you should consider the simplest, most natural solutions first. More extreme eradication methods such as pesticides can have serious consequences on other beneficial organisms in the soil, as well as affecting people who use the lawn and nearby natural resources such as water tables. Besides, there are so many natural treatments that chances are you can solve your problems without ever turning to synthetic insecticides or pesticides.

Not all evidence of insect damage is as apparent as the sawdust-like residue left by billbugs. Normally, you'll need to see the insect itself.

Integrated Pest Management ▸

Integrated Pest Management (IPM) is a relatively new concept in lawn care and gardening. Focused on environmentally beneficial practices in pest control, it involves viewing the yard as a complete ecosystem where anything you do to one living organism affects all the other organisms. The concept clearly lays out four guiding criteria, including:

- **Action thresholds,** or the point at which the number of pests or the amount of damage indicates the need for some action. In lawn care, this translates to determining if the damage or pest population you've detected is modest enough that you should take a wait-and-see attitude, or if you need to take action to prevent further damage to your lawn. Small spot problems may not be worth treating aggressively.
- **Monitor and Identify.** Where IPM is concerned—and where sound lawn-care pest control is concerned—it's essential to see and understand what's happening, and verify that the pest you think is causing the damage is actually causing the damage.

- **Prevention.** This is the first step in dealing with pests, and can include changing fertilizer schedules to slow down growth so that harmful insects will view the lawn less favorably, and seeding with different grass species that the insects you're dealing with don't like.
- **Control.** This comes last, once you've definitively identified the pest, determined the extent of the damage, and attempted whatever form of prevention might be available to you. Taking action to control the pests begins with the least risky and least toxic solution first, working toward more powerful alternatives only after the initial attempts at control or eradication prove unsuccessful.

Although IPM was developed as a more ecologically focused way to solve pest problems, the method includes the possible use of chemical pesticides. This means it is not considered an organic process by organic gardeners. Just the same, it is a sound method, and a good one for the homeowner to follow in attacking a lawn pest problem.

Natural Pest Controls

Insects are attracted to your lawn because it offers them something they want. If you make the lawn a less hospitable place, sometimes that takes care of the problem. The two most common conditions in a lawn that draw harmful insects are a thick layer of thatch and persistent moisture. Dethatching your lawn not only improves overall lawn health, it can also take away the habitat of insects that are causing other problems. Likewise, if you simply improve your watering routine or increase drainage in wet areas of the lawn, you'll be taking steps to deny refuge to moisture-loving insects. Biological controls are your next point of attack. Typically, this means increasing the population of beneficial organisms that prey on harmful insects.

Beneficial nematodes—microorganisms that have an appetite for the larvae of many lawn pests—are one of the most common biological controls. They will aggressively attack and destroy common white grubs, cutworm and sod webworm larvae, army worms, and other pests. Nematodes, sold in bags containing several million of the microscopic roundworms, are also easy to install. They are mixed with lukewarm water and then applied to the problem area or even broadcast across the entire lawn. The lawn should be thoroughly moist before nematodes are applied. If you can, wait until the sun sets to apply nematodes—direct sunlight can sterilize them. Nematodes are at their most effective and aggressive when the soil temperature is between 65 and 90°F.

Bacillus thuringiensis, known as BT, is another common and effective biological control. The many different strains of this bacteria are used in applications from vegetable gardens to lawns (when you purchase BT you want to make sure you're buying the strain applicable to the insects you're fighting). BT is effective against white grubs, sod webworms and other harmful worms, and is available at most large, well-stocked garden centers and nurseries. It must be kept refrigerated before use, should be mixed with water according to the package instructions, and applied with a sprayer. One application rarely kills the entire population of insects you're trying to eradicate, so be prepared to reapply as necessary every two weeks.

Endophytes are another way to fight detrimental insects. The microscopic endophyte fungi infect the grass without hurting it, but make blades and

White grubs are one of the most common lawn pests, and one of the most easily eradicated with organic controls.

Nematodes are microscopic organisms (parasitic worms, actually) that attack several insects that can damage your lawn, including lawn grubs, cutworms, and slugs.

leaf stalks toxic to insects such as chinch bugs, sod webworms and billbugs. This is a longer-term solution because you'll need to overseed with grass seed that has been inoculated with endophytes. Once those seeds begin growing, the insects begin dying. Only a limited number of grass species are available as inoculated seeds, mostly comprising cool-season grasses.

Botanical insecticides are derived from plant sources, so they break down quickly after use and are fairly harmless to humans and animals. Neem is one of the most common. Derived from a tropical tree, it can kill immature feeding insects and has been known to repel Japanese beetles so that they cannot lay the eggs that result in white grubs.

Pyrethin is a common organic insecticide, derived from the daisy. It is a broad-spectrum insecticide that should be used carefully because it can kill both beneficial and harmful insects. It's best used as a spot treatment for localized infestations of sod webworms or white grubs. It is sometimes combined with synthetic additives to amplify its effects and power, and doing so can make it toxic to other insects such as armyworms and aphids, although it can also become toxic to beneficial insects and harmful to the environment.

Rotenone is extracted from an Asian plant. It has long been used as a broad-spectrum insecticide that is slow to work and also somewhat dangerous for pets and humans.

All of these solutions—or a combination—can be highly effective. Most of these work slower than chemical insecticides and on a more limited range of insects in many cases. But the trade-off is that they do minimal damage and are environmentally responsible. In the end, one or more of these treatments can solve just about any insect problem you'll encounter in your lawn.

Bacillus thuringiensis is a natural bacteria that is used to combat caterpillars and some types of worms that damage lawns.

Diatomaceous Earth ▸

Made from the ground up fossils of ancient plants called diatoms, diatomaceous earth is a highly effective and completely organic insecticide. The material is a fine dust that doesn't harm humans or animals, but slices the outer skin that serves as a skeleton for most insects, or shreds their digestive systems. You should use only agricultural- or food-grade diatomaceous earth (there's a more harmful type used for pool filtration), and dust it over any lawn area with an insect problem. You can spread it by hand, or with a spreader over larger areas. Either way, you should wear a high-quality dust mask when you are working with diatomaceous earth. It usually works within 48 hours. It's most effective against ants and aphids, although it will harm many types of top-dwelling insects. It can also harm beneficial insects, so it should not be used as a regular preventative treatment.

Diatomaceous earth is the active ingredient in this natural insecticide product.

Beneficial Insects

One of the best ways to eradicate harmful pests is by enticing their natural predators into your yard. These beneficial insects can be the best, most ecological solution to solving pest problems in the lawn. Although you can actually buy and introduce species such as lady beetles, the best way to bring in the good guys is by creating an environment they find attractive. This usually means adding a diversity of flowering plants, and a water source doesn't hurt either. The more diverse your yard and garden, the more diverse the insect population will be—including a range of beneficials (as well as birds that feast on grubs!).

If you want to foster populations of beneficial insects, you should also limit the chemical controls you use in the lawn. Pesticides of any sort may drive away or kill beneficial insects as quickly as they do the harmful types. The more chemicals you introduce for whatever reason, the more you put insect populations at risk.

Some of the beneficial insects that you should keep any eye out for include:

Lady beetles. Popularly known as lady bugs, these easily recognized insects are the groundskeeper's friend (although some species, such as the Japanese Lady Beetle, can overrun your home). The lady beetle feasts on aphids and other soft-bodied insects. The larvae, especially, are hungry eaters that can put a huge dent in detrimental insect populations.

Ground beetle. Don't make the mistake of trying to eliminate this ugly friend. The ground beetle with its iridescent body and spindly black legs won't win any beauty contests, but it will eat grubs, armyworms, and cutworms.

Braconid wasps. Are tiny creatures that lay eggs inside of their prey or in the pupal cocoons of the prey larvae. In this way, they destroy aphids, grubs, and other insects.

Lady beetle

Ground beetle

Braconid wasp

The lady beetle is one of the most effective beneficial insects any homeowner can hope for, feasting on a range of lawn-damaging pests.

Lacewing

Lacewing. Named for its distinctive, delicate gossamer wings, the lacewing may look like a fragile beauty, but they're anything but dainty when it comes to attacking aphids. In fact, their larvae are sometimes known as "aphid lions" for an almost insatiable appetite. The larvae will also eat other harmful insects in the egg stage.

Big-eyed bugs. Appropriately named for their bulging eyes, these insects are a feared enemy of chinch bugs. They are tiny and green in the east, and brown in the west of North America. But no matter where they call home, they go after chinch bugs, leafhoppers, aphids, and caterpillars.

Big-eyed bug

Using Pesticides ▸

Chemical pesticides and insecticides should be the options of last resort when you're dealing with an insect problem in the lawn. Although pesticide companies formulate their products to be as safe as possible, the fact remains that any synthetic pesticide is potentially harmful to animals and humans, and they have the potential to damage the environment as well.

Proper pesticide usage begins with identifying exactly the insect you're trying to eradicate. Once you're certain of the species, the next step is to read pesticide labels closely and completely. The law sets out stringent requirements for pesticide manufacturers and outlines what they must include on the label. You'll find relevant safety information along with a list of insects the pesticide is used to treat. Only use a pesticide if the insect you're targeting is listed. Pesticides are also labeled for use on either warm- or cool-season lawns. Don't use it if it is recommended for a different season than your lawn.

Pesticide regulations cover the user as well as the manufacturer. You are legally obligated to use pesticides in a safe manner in accordance to the manufacturer's instructions and prevailing best standards and practices. Pay particular attention to dosing. Using exactly the recommended amount of pesticide is a key step in insect eradication. More is not better, nor is too little.

Apply granular pesticides just as you would spread fertilizer, but use a drop spreader, not a broadcast or hand-held model. Spray liquid formulas with a hose end sprayer for pre-mixed types, and a pressure sprayer for concentrated liquid pesticides. Never apply pesticide when it's raining or about to rain, or on windy days.

Clean all equipment thoroughly after use, rinsing it several times and allowing it to dry thoroughly. If you use a sprayer for herbicides or other applications, it's a good idea to use a separate one for pesticides, because even after rinsing, some residue remains.

Follow all instructions to the letter and use commonsense safety practices, and you'll quickly eradicate the detrimental insects. Always follow up, though, with healthy lawn maintenance to create an environment that discourages a recurrence of the pest.

Pesticides are some of the most dangerous chemicals you'll ever use in your yard, so take every precaution necessary to apply them in the safest way possible.

- Wear appropriate clothing, including long pants, a long-sleeve shirt, sturdy shoes, and rubber gloves.
- Protect your lungs. Wear a high-quality dust mask when dusting with pesticide, and a tight-fitting respirator when spraying it. Look for specific masks approved by the National Institute for Safety and Health (NIOSH).
- Clean up completely. Thoroughly rinse equipment and rubber gloves, and wash the clothes you used during application in a load by themselves.
- Choose your product carefully. Use the pesticide with the least risks and side effects, and the one most targeted to the insect you need to eradicate.
- Store pesticides properly. They should be locked up in a cabinet out of the reach of children.
- Dispose of leftover, out-of-date pesticide according to local sanitation codes.
- Keep all pesticides in their original containers.

Common Problem Insects

This photo guide will help you identify the culprit you're dealing with in diagnosing lawn damage. Keep in mind that some insects are nocturnal, and have to be detected at night—a flashlight and patience will be your best friends in this type of detective work. Some underground enemies, such as grubs, are visible only when you lift an area of the lawn. Once you've identified the villain, follow the steps listed to eradicate them.

BLACK ANTS & FIRE ANTS

Black ants are generally beneficial to a lawn's ecology, but may become a problem when colonies grow large and several anthills appear. Although they are limited to certain areas of the deep south and a few locations in the north of the country, fire ants are a much greater nuisance than black ants. They build bigger hills in the lawn than other species do, and they are far more aggressive. Fire ants will swarm pets and humans alike, causing painful stings that can lead to anaphylactic shock.

Treatment: You can get rid of the black anthills by physically destroying them and raking them out, or pouring boiling water into them. If the problem persists, and becomes overwhelming, turn to an age-old remedy of borax (boric acid) mixed with sugar—although make sure no small children or pets will be in the area. Make an effective boric acid trap by forming a hollow ball out of several layers of aluminum foil, filling it with a borax-and-sugar mix, and punching small holes in it.

To get rid of fire ants, use spinosad, a natural botanical pesticide that is broadcast around the fire ant hill in spring or fall.

Chinch bug (nymph)

CHINCH BUGS

One of the most common lawn pests, chinch bugs have tiny black bodies and white wings. The females lay eggs in late spring or early summer, which hatch into a stage called nymphs. The red nymphs cause most of the damage to grass plants by sucking juices from the grass blades, leaving toxins in their place, and creating round, yellow patches in sunny parts of the lawn. The nymphs tend to cause damage in the middle of summer in cool-season lawns, and in late spring in warm-season lawns.

Treatment: Dealing with chinch bugs begins with regular lawn watering. The insects proliferate in drought conditions, and don't like moist soil. You can also treat them with insecticidal soaps, applied in liquid solution over the affected area. This treatment may need to be repeated to completely eradicate the infestation. You can also spot treat with pyrethin.

SOD WEBWORMS

The first sign of sod webworms is usually the adult moths that appear over your lawn in spring during the early evening. The moths lay eggs that hatch two to three weeks later. Signs that the larvae are causing damage include small sections of dead grass about the size of a drink coaster. The detrimental larvae are just under an inch long, with black-spotted grey bodies. The larvae burrow into thatch during the day, and feed on blades of grass during the evening.

Fire ant

Sod webworm

White grub

Treatment: Like many lawn pests, sod webworms infiltrate and thrive in poorly maintained lawns, which makes improving the health of your lawn the first step in treating an infestation. Dethatching will remove the hiding places for the destructive larvae. Beneficial nematodes are extremely effective against the larvae, especially when applied shortly after they hatch. Turn to BT and pyrethrin for severe infestations on which other solutions have not worked.

BILLBUGS

Adult billbugs are tiny beetle-like insects, but the threat to your lawn is posed by the larvae. The white grubs with orange heads eat the blades of grass, causing small areas of dead lawn, much like you would see with sod webworm larvae. However, billbug larvae leave a sawdust-like scattering of waste product near the crown of a grass plant. The larvae are most active and destructive in the middle of summer.

Treatment: As with other grubs, the first line of defense is a healthy lawn, specifically a lack of thatch. Dethatching is the first step in treatment of billbug infestations. The botanical insecticides neem and rotenone are effective, as is insecticidal soap. You can also turn to beneficial nematodes to eradicate obvious infestations.

WHITE GRUBS

These ubiquitous insects are actually the larvae of Japanese beetles, along with a few other beetle types. If you find beetles on your roses or vegetables, chances are you have some level of white grub problem that can result in extensive damage to grass plant roots. The grubs sever the roots from the plant, causing dead patches and bare areas in spring. As if that weren't enough, grubs are an irresistible attraction to burrowing predators, like moles and skunks.

Treatment: The most common and effective treatment for killing Japanese beetle white grubs is milky spore. Other species can be treated with beneficial nematodes.

MOLE CRICKETS

The mole cricket can easily be mistaken for the common cricket. The difference is that the mole cricket has a larger head with thicker front legs—and it is much more destructive. Feeding on grass plant roots, it tunnels under the soil, creating significant cavities that can cause the lawn to feel spongy underfoot. An infestation will be quite apparent; aside from the tunnels, the crickets are pretty nonchalant about appearing openly in the grass.

Billbug

Mole cricket

Common cricket

Treatment: Beneficial nematodes are effective against mole cricket eggs, but this control needs to be applied with fairly precise timing to kill the crickets before they hatch. Neem is also somewhat effective, as long as it is watered into the soil deeply.

APHIDS

Also known as greenbugs, these are tiny, nearly transparent insects that are hard to detect without careful examination. They suck the fluids out of grass blades (and many other garden plants), while injecting a toxin that eventually kills the plant. Grass will slowly turn brown in small areas under an aphid attack.

Treatment: Aphids are a favorite food of many different beneficial insects. They can also be washed off the grass with a vigorous blast of water. If you have a widespread infestation, you can use an application of insecticidal soap.

CUTWORMS

Common to colder parts of the country, cutworms often migrate from vegetable or flower gardens to the lawn. They are actually caterpillars (the larvae of moths) and are plenty ugly, with plump and dark brown or black bodies. They are nocturnal and feed on grass blades in one area, causing circular dead spots in the lawn. Generally, you should treat them aggressively if there are more than 5 or 6 worms in a square yard of sod.

Treatment: BT is the solution of choice for cutworm infestations, although beneficial nematodes and pyrethin spray are also very effective.

Aphids

Cutworm

Thinking Green: Oil's Well ▶

When it comes to repelling unwanted inhabitants in your lawn, you can turn to nature's own defenses—specifically, plant oils. For instance, castor oil made from the seeds of the castor bean plant can be applied to the soil to send moles and voles packing. Rosemary oil can be combined with pure peppermint oil to create an insecticide that fights chinch bugs. Peppermint oil can also be combined with clove oil to create a nerve toxin that is fatal to many insects. Orange peel extract is used in several natural insecticide sprays because it tends to degrade and destroy the respiratory systems of several insect species. When it comes to defending plants—including the grass plants that make up your lawn—few formulations can beat nature's own.

Getting Rid of Skunks and Raccoons

Normally, skunks, raccoons, and (in the south) armadillos cause few problems for the average lawn. There simply isn't much of interest to lure these mammals into your yard. That is, until they discover that a treasure trove of grubs is easily accessible just below the surface of the sod.

That's when the trouble starts. Even if the grubs themselves aren't causing much damage, you'll suddenly find sections of sod pulled up, with the soil underneath tilled. It may be a mystery until you realize that these wild raiders tend to eat at night or very early in the morning.

You can build a fence or try one of several home remedies such as motion-activated safety lights, or predator urine. But don't count on these solutions. Raccoons are wily and tend not to be put off by light or noise, while skunks are generally fearless for good reason (sharp claws and a unique defense mechanism).

In the end, if you have an ongoing problem that you can trace to any of these three animals, the only real permanent way to dissuade them from digging up your lawn is to send them to greener pastures. If you eradicate your grub population, these animals have little reason to visit your lawn, or dig it up. If you spot raccoons or skunks in your city yard, notify animal control immediately, because there is a good chance that they are rabid, hurt, or otherwise dangerous. Never attempt to handle or deal with a wild animal that seems disoriented or aggressive.

When the Pest is a Pet ▶

If you're not walking your dog regularly, he will probably choose a part of your lawn on which to do his business, and he'll return to the same spot again and again. If you notice a spot on the lawn that grows rapidly and turns dark green and then brown, your pet is probably the culprit. To fix pet damage, flush the spot thoroughly with water, repeating in subsequent days. To allow the grass to return, you'll have to get into a schedule of walking your dog, or train him or her to go on another surface off the lawn.

Skunks and other hungry mammals can do plenty of damage to your lawn in their quest for delicious grubs.

Dealing with Tunneling Rodents

In most cases, wildlife will avoid your lawn. After all, it's an exposed area with little in the way of protective cover. Plus, a healthy lawn offers a dearth of tempting dinner items. But when you have grubs or other insects in your lawn, they may attract other visitors. The most common of these are moles, voles, and gophers.

Moles. Moles tunnel under the lawn in search of grubs. Left alone, they will clear your lawn of white grub infestations, but they'll also leave behind unsightly tunnels that make the lawn a challenge to mow. Experts are somewhat divided on how big of a problem moles really are. Because they're meat-eaters, they don't actually consume any of your lawn. However, they do damage the lawn by raising the sod, and they can also traumatize grass roots in their tunneling. Because they are solitary animals, any mole problem you have is usually limited to a single rodent.

You can tamp down the tunnels and water well to make sure roots reestablish after they've been disturbed by the mole. Getting rid of the mole entails a two-part strategy. Treating the lawn with beneficial nematodes or other applicable product to eradicate the grubs is the first part. With the grubs gone, the mole may leave for other feeding grounds. However, if he stays around to feast on your earthworms, you may want to trap him.

You can live-trap a mole and then transport it to a wild area such as a state or national park. If that is too much hassle and you see the mole as just a nuisance and an undesirable varmint, you can use a kill trap, which requires less effort—you simply throw away the trap and dead animal when the trap is successful. You can also bait for moles, although this is not a good idea if you have pets or children around—even if they are just casual visitors to your house. Bait lasts a long time and you don't want any but the target animal consuming it.

Gophers. Gophers are similar to moles in that they tunnel throughout the yard in search of food, although the food they are looking for is plant matter. They don't usually feed on grass roots, but the search to find a tasty meal will often take them beneath your lawn, causing damage similar to what a busy mole will leave behind. Gophers travel in larger groups and can be a persistent problem, and are usually trapped. However, if you can locate active tunnels, sponges soaked with ammonia placed in the tunnels will cause the gopher to vacate to another area. Just remember to remove the sponges once that gopher has left.

Voles. Voles differ from moles in that they regularly surface (moles only emerge by accident). Among voles, the pine vole is a burrower and a threat to your grass roots. The non-burrowing meadow vole is a threat in the cooler months, when it will chew uncut grass down to the roots as a cold-weather source of nutrition.

Regardless of which type you're dealing with, the best method to eradicate voles is trapping. Use a large rat trap if you don't mind killing the animal; live-trap and relocate it if you do. Peanut butter is an effective bait for these animals either way. But tackle the problem early, because unlike moles and gophers, voles are quick to reproduce and colonize.

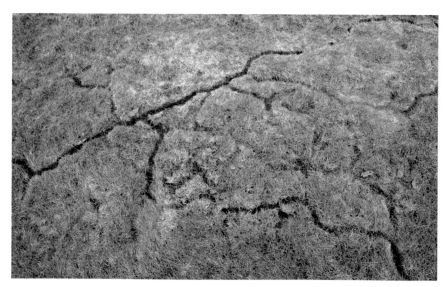

By the time you see evidence of a mole, gopher, or vole, a lot of damage has already been done—quick action is necessary to stop large-scale devastation of the lawn. The best way to find active tunnels for any burrowing rodent is to get up very early in the morning and watch the tops of the tunnels for movement. You can also mark tunnels, and check later to determine if the marks have been disturbed.

The Underground Trio

Moles have a distinctive appearance, with shortened forelimbs equipped with oversized digging claws, no visible ears, and tiny, nearly non-existent eye slits.

Voles have a mouse-like appearance, with small but obvious ears, prominent tiny eyes, and reddish brown or grey fur.

Gophers are distinguishable by their large teeth, whiskers, and the pouches on either side of the mouth.

Sonic Warfare ▸

You'll find a host of high-tech products on the market that claim to repel any burrowing rodent in your yard. The idea is to stick a probe into the ground or set speakers down that produce sonic, ultrasonic, or electromagnetic energy. The energy is in the form of high-pitched noise or waves. Manufacturers claim that the energy drives the rodents out of their mind and out of your yard. Unfortunately, the claims remain largely unproven, and professional groundskeepers have not had a great deal of success in using these devices. Until more quantitative proof is produced regarding these devices, it generally makes sense to use time-tested remedies such as traps or tunnel flooding.

Dealing With Lawn Diseases

It's a simple fact that lawn diseases don't just pop up out of thin air. The disease itself can be present, having arrived from any number of sources, including airborne, bird borne, animal borne—it may even have arrived on tools or equipment brought from elsewhere and used in the yard. But no matter where it came from, for the disease to take hold, it needs a hospitable breeding environment and a grass that is susceptible to the disease. The lawn usually has several problems that serve to create the right conditions for growth of the disease.

The key to treating any disease in your lawn is first correctly identifying it. This can be a challenge because many lawn diseases look very similar to other conditions, such as drought, nitrogen burn, or pet spotting. Take a close look not only at the damaged grass, but also at the overall pattern of destruction. Look at the grass around the damaged area and check for any changes in the healthy grass. Inspect individual blades to determine if they have any particular marks on them, and check different areas of the lawn to determine if there are different stages of the same disease at work.

If the disease is not fairly obvious, but it is widespread, you may need help in identifying and treating it. You can talk to a local nursery professional who may have encountered other customers with the same problem. Or, if you want to go a little more in depth, contact your local cooperative extension office. The experts there may be able to give you information on the disease you're dealing with, as well as possible courses of treatment. As a last resort, if you're having no success in fighting the disease, you can take a sod sample to the extension office. Ask them for a referral to a lab that can analyze the disease.

ROOT CAUSES OF LAWN DISEASE

- Most lawn diseases are water-related. Some diseases thrive in a very moist habitat, while others will do best in arid surroundings. Either way, few diseases do well in a lawn that is irrigated at just the right time with just the right amount of water for the climate and the type of grass.

- Improper mowing is a common mistake that invites diseases to take hold. The height you mow should reflect the type of grass you're mowing (see page 122 for ideal heights according to different species). Mowing consistently too low or too infrequently, or using a mower with a dull blade, are examples of improper mowing that can lead to lawn disease.

- Disease can take hold in the lawn if you have a dense, thick layer of thatch. The more thatch there is, the more disease spores it can harbor.

- How, when, and how much you fertilize and use insecticides or pesticides will also affect the lawn's resistance to disease. The more chemicals used on the lawn, the greater the chance that disease-fighting beneficial organisms will be killed.

Need Some Expert Help? ▸

You local agricultural extension office is the best source for assistance in identifying and combating lawn disease. These local agencies are part of a larger network called the Cooperative Extension System. This network is partnered with the National Institute of Food and Agriculture (NIFA), which is administered by the U.S. Department of Agriculture. Although the NIFA has some helpful resources, its primary benefit for homeowners is as a clearinghouse for local agencies. By logging on to their website you can easily find contact information for the agricultural extension closest to you—often a division of a land grant university. The website address is: www.nifa.usda.gov/Extension/.

Treating Lawn Diseases

Quick fixes are hard to come by once a disease has taken hold in your lawn, which is why most experts preach prevention. Fungicides are available for individual diseases and can be effective in certain cases, but as with most strong chemicals, there are repercussions to using fungicides. The most important is that the chemicals can kill good fungi at the same time as bad. Some fungicides are long-lasting, lingering in the soil long after they've served their purpose. That's why fungicides are generally considered the option of last resort for treating most lawn diseases. More often, the answer lies in changing one of the three legs of lawn disease "triangle": susceptible grass species, conditions that foster disease, and the presence of disease spores.

You can overseed with a resistant grass, but that's a long-term solution. Changing the conditions in the lawn is the more immediate treatment. This includes being fastidious about watering, and getting rid of thatch. To treat the spores themselves, consider topdressing with compost. Certain specific types of compost have been linked to disease eradication. These include composted manures, leaf composts, and sludge compost such as Milorganite. Ultimately, it pays to remember that the lawn has its own disease-fighting mechanisms and the healthier you keep it, the better equipped it is to respond to an infection. That's why you may want to take a wait-and-see approach if the outbreak does not seem severe, making sure that your lawn care practices are as painstaking as possible.

Dollar spot is one of many common fungal ailments that afflict lawns. As with most lawn diseases, a change in how you water and care for the lawn is usually the best course of action to eradicate the disease naturally.

Survival of the Fittest ▸

The type of grass in your lawn impacts how resistant the lawn will be to diseases. Some species are naturally disease resistant to certain conditions. But grass seed companies are constantly developing new varieties that are more tolerant to adverse circumstances such as drought, and are resistant to specific diseases. Consider disease resistance part of your purchase decision if you're buying sod or seed for a new lawn, or for overseeding. The professionals at local nurseries, garden centers, and your local cooperative extension office will be able to instruct you on diseases that are common in your area, and the latest resistant grass varieties available.

Lawn Disease Identification & Treatment

If you're going to fight a lawn disease, you need to know which one you're fighting. Identification is key and the photos shown here will give you a better idea of exactly what each disease looks like. The listings here represent the most common lawn diseases, along with treatments to eradicate them, repair their damage, and prevent them from recurring.

BROWN PATCH

This soil-borne fungus is a common problem in regions where high humidity combines with warm temperatures. Grasses most often affected by the disease include Kentucky bluegrass, centipede grass, Bermuda grass, and St. Augustine. The disease is usually most active in late spring and early fall for warm-season grasses, and early spring for cool-season types. The fungus attacks while the grass is actively growing. Onset is encouraged by overfertilization and overwatering. The first signs of brown patch are small circles of wet-looking grass that quickly turn brown. The damaged patch enlarges quickly, but eventually the infected area begins to return to health, creating rings of brown that are lined on the outside by yellowing grass, sometimes called a "smoke ring." Infected areas can range from the size of a dinner plate to many feet in diameter. You may, in certain instances, notice lesions on the grass leaves. The lesions will be brown, going black at the edges.

Treatment: Lawns can recover from brown patch in time, especially when measures are taken to correct the conditions that allow the fungus to thrive in the first place. Water only in the morning and only when the lawn absolutely needs it. Mow the lawn higher than normal, and cut back on fertilization. Aerate as necessary and alleviate pockets of deep shade on the lawn if you can. If your lawn has been affected by the fungus before, or if you know that it is common in your area, you can treat with a preventative fungicide in early spring (although this usually isn't necessary).

FAIRY RINGS

Fairy rings are one of the most distinctive lawn diseases, characterized by rings of lush lawn growth, often accompanied by growth of mushrooms along the ring (and sometimes featuring just mushrooms in the ring formation without the underlying excessive lawn growth). Fairy rings sometimes include dieback in the ring formation if the fungus is so prolific as to block water absorption by the grass. But more often, the grass survives. The fungus usually returns the next year, often creating a larger ring. It's caused by decaying organic matter that contained the fungus to start with, usually added as a soil amendment when the lawn was first planted.

Treatment: Because the effects are largely to the appearance and not the health of the lawn, fairy rings are usually treated as a cosmetic problem. Remove the mushrooms (which are toxic, so you should keep children away from them). Water and fertilize as usual. Eradication of the fungus entails digging out the infected area and removing soil and sod as deep as 10 inches—which is why most homeowners simply cover up the disease's affects. There are powerful fungicides for use on the fungi that cause fairy rings, but these are not considered safe for home lawn use.

A lawn with brown patch

Fairy rings

Pythium blight

PYTHIUM BLIGHT

The first signs of pythium blight, or grease spot as it is sometimes called, are small dark areas that may look slimy or greasy. The affected area can range from around 1 inch to over a foot in diameter. The disease spreads rapidly, creating signature reddish brown and wilted grass sections that may streak as the disease follows the lines of drainage. Infected grass will shrivel and turn brown. The appearance may include a cotton web-like growth, especially in the evening and early morning.

Treatment: Fight the disease with fungicide as soon as you notice an outbreak. Prevention is key, involving aerating to improve drainage and, specifically, correcting any alkalinity imbalance with an application of lime, as necessary.

SNOW MOLD

As the name implies, this fungus only occurs in colder areas of the country with freezing temperatures and snow. The fungus grows under cover of the snow, in wet conditions, and is more prone to shady areas in which the snow melts late.

There are actually two types: pink and gray. Both appear as patches of dead, brown grass surrounded on the margins by a gray or pinkish fuzzy growth. Gray snow mold is the less damaging of the two, affecting only the blades of the grass. Pink snow mold infects the blades and crown, and can do serious damage to the lawn.

Treatment: The fungicides effective on snow molds are not recommended for home use. Generally, the treatment consists of changing the conditions that fuel the fungus. These changes include cutting the lawn short for winterization, forgoing nitrogen-rich fertilizer in the fall, and improving drainage through dethatching and aeration.

LEAF SPOT

Leaf spot is also called "melting out," which actually describes the second, more destructive effect of the disease. The first signs are spot-like lesions on the grass leaves. The lesions resemble burns, with brown centers and darkened margins. These symptoms appear in early spring or fall, and cause no serious damage to the grass. However, the second phase of the disease—melting out—involves the fungus moving into the crown and roots of affected grass plants, killing them. This happens in the hottest weather of the summer.

Treatment: Apply a contact fungicide at the first signs of leaf spot, and expect to reapply until the signs disappear. Usually, three or four applications spaced a week apart are necessary. Prevention focuses on avoiding overfertilization, and watering deeply once or twice per week, in the early morning, to prevent water from sitting on the grass leaves. Keep in mind when overseeding that there are many new varieties of leaf spot-resistant grasses.

Snow mold

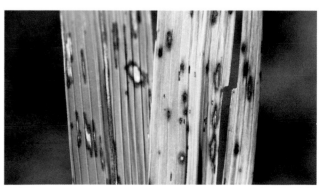

Leaf spot

DOLLAR SPOT

Dollar spot is one of the lawn diseases that mimic the look of many other conditions. It's named after the silver-dollar size dead spots the fungus creates in the lawn. However, the spots are often larger than that, and can develop into significant areas of dead grass. The disease is most common during spring and fall, when the weather is the mild 60 to 80°F range that the fungus thrives in. In some regions it will persist through summer. The fungus is spread throughout the lawn by contact with shoes, sprinklers, hoses, and lawn-care equipment.

Treatment: If the infection is widespread, use contact fungicide labeled for dollar spot at the first sign of outbreak, and repeat the application a week to 10 days after the first treatment. To prevent dollar spot from returning, you should water only in the morning and ensure that the lawn is receiving the proper nutrients. Overseed the lawn with resistant varieties. Ultimately, however, your lawn will recover on it's own from an attack of dollar spot, although it may take months for the lawn to completely regenerate.

Dollar spot

POWDERY MILDEW

This fungus exhibits a distinctive coating on the top growth of the lawn, resembling a dusting of powdered sugar or flour. The mildew coating ranges from white to gray, and only in severe cases will it actually kill the grass. The fungus prefers shaded sections of the lawn in regions with cool nights and high humidity. It is most common in lawns of Kentucky bluegrass, although other grasses may be affected as well.

Treatment: Mildew is regularly treated with a broad-spectrum systemic fungicide at the first signs of outbreak, with a repeat application around a week later. To prevent recurrence, prune shrubs and trees to allow more sunlight exposure over shaded areas of the lawn, and water only moderately in affected areas.

Powdery mildew

RUST

This aptly named fungus coats grass blades with orange and reddish brown spores that can be rubbed off. It most commonly afflicts Kentucky bluegrass and perennial ryegrass, and strikes in late summer and early fall. Outbreaks occur most often in lawns already stressed by other conditions or diseases. The fungus grows best in mildly warm, moist conditions.

Treatment: In most cases, rust will cause only minimal cosmetic damage, with no significant grass die-off. If you detect the disease, continue to mow regularly, bagging and disposing of the clippings. In severe cases, treat the lawn with a systemic fungicide, repeating the application in a week as necessary.

Rust

Red thread

RED THREAD

The namesake pink and red strands of this fungus attach to leaves and sheaths of the grass plant, causing irregular die-off and a ragged lawn appearance. From a distance, the disease in full bloom may give the lawn a reddish hue. The fungus is active in cool, moist weather in early spring and fall. In the vast majority of cases, the disease causes no serious long-term damage to the lawn.

Treatment: Red thread may be a sign of potassium deficiency that should be corrected with organic or synthetic fertilizer, after being confirmed with a soil test. Water sparingly, and only in the morning. In very extreme cases, apply a contact fungicide labeled for use on red thread.

LEAF SMUT

There are two types of leaf smuts that affect lawns: stripe smut and flag smut. When infected with either fungus, grass will turn pale yellow, followed by long gray-black streaks on the grass blades. Smuts thrive in the cool weather of early spring or fall. The grass blades will wither and die, and the fungus eventually moves into the crown and other tissues in the plant. Plants often die as the summer warms.

Treatment: Leaf smuts, like many fungi, flourish in deep, dense thatch. They also grow best in acidic soil with an abundance of nitrogen. That's why dethatching and fertilizing lightly are the first steps in limiting the effects of leaf smuts. Severe cases can be treated with systemic fungicides, but the wisest course of action is to simply reseed damaged areas with one of the many disease-resistant cultivars.

FUSARIUM BLIGHT

Sometimes called summer patch, this fungus grows most actively in hot weather above 85°F and in drought-stressed lawns. It appears as small circles of graying or brown dead or dying grass. The best way to tell fusarium blight from other conditions with similar symptoms is to examine the crowns of dead plants—they often feature a reddish rot.

Treatment: Maintaining proper mowing height is crucial in prevention, as is keeping the lawn consistently moist through hot and arid periods. There are also a number of blight-resistant cultivars that should be used to overseed lawns that have proven susceptible to attack. As a last resort, apply an appropriate contact fungicide.

Leaf smut

Fusarium blight

Improving Site Conditions

In a perfect world, your lawn would sit atop a deep layer of loam and bask in a wealth of sunshine and ideal temperatures. The lawn would slope gently, almost imperceptibly, creating efficient, non-eroding drainage for whatever excess water the lawn received. In the real world, there are very few perfect places for lawns.

The fact is, if your yard is fairly large—and even if it isn't—chances are that the lawn will have one or more trouble spots or challenging areas where it's hard to keep the grass healthy. Some site-related problems are easily fixed, while others call for more creative solutions.

One of the most common inhibitors to thick, lush turf is shade. Shade is a reality for many mature landscapes where shrubs have grown tall and the canopies of long-established trees arch over whole areas of the lawn. The trick is in opening up those screens as much as possible, and in ensuring watering and mowing practices don't make the situation worse.

Drainage is another key issue for any lawn. The soil composition will control drainage to a certain degree, but the topography of your lawn will also influence how quickly water makes its way through the lawn and where, why, and how it collects. Ensuring proper drainage can involve solutions from the simple, such as slowly improving the soil by top-dressing, to the complex, such as installing a French drain. The solution that you choose will be guided by how serious and extensive your drainage issues are.

Drainage can involve grading the soil and landscape, but grading may also be required for different features in the lawn. For instance, if you are adding a child's play structure or putting green, you may need to grade that particular area differently then the rest of the lawn.

Lastly, your site location and particular features may lead you to make aesthetic improvements. For instance, installing edging between the lawn border and the line of a flower or shrub bed will provide a crisp look to the lawn, but it also may be necessary to prevent aggressive species such as ivies or other ground covers from invading your lawn.

The point is, by proactively responding to the challenges posed by your site, you can head off a lot of problems before they begin. It's one more way to ensure a healthy, trouble-free lawn.

A severe slope can be an unusable and hard-to-maintain area of a lawn. A few simple terraces create an attractive, low-maintenance yard feature instead.

Deep shade such as this can lead to a host of lawn problems, from poor grass growth to a proliferation of lawn diseases. The solution is to prune trees judiciously, to thin out sun-blocking canopies.

Certain types of gardens, such as native perennial beds, contain fairly aggressive plants that will covet your turf space and eventually make a play for it. You can keep most of them at bay with simple lawn edging.

Dealing With Shaded Areas

Shade is a hard thing to plan for. Trees that were relatively young when your lawn was planted often grow to become incredible sun blockers. Or you may have made your lawn-care plan in the winter, when the trees surrounding your yard were bare of leaves, not realizing that in season they were going to create dense dark areas inhospitable to grass growth.

Areas of deep or persistent shade call for a change in lawn-care tactics. The challenge is changing the way you care for one small area of lawn, while maintaining the proper maintenance for the rest of the yard. That can be a bit of bother, but if you're going to keep shaded grass healthy, you need to make adjustments.

The first is in how you feed shaded parts of the lawn. You may want to skip any mid-season feedings in the shady areas, because those feedings will divert resources of already challenged grass from roots to top growth. Shaded top growth is already full of moisture, so adding denser leaves means attracting insects and disease that prefer moist environments. It's best for shaded areas of grass to be fertilized in spring and fall when deciduous trees are leafless. When winterizing a shady area, use a potassium-heavy fertilizer to fortify the grass against the stress of its location.

Watering is also important. Shaded areas need less water than other areas of the lawn, and allowing consistently moist conditions in a shady part of the lawn is simply asking for insect and disease problems. Check that shaded portions are regularly drying out before watering.

Overseed the problem area with shade-tolerant species and varieties. This is a simple way to introduce a more appropriate strain of grass over time.

You can also approach the problem from the other side of the equation, by increasing the sunlight in the area. This usually entails pruning back shrubs and trees that are keeping the lawn in shadow. In some cases, where a significant portion of the lawn has suffered under the shade of a large tree, you may want remove the tree if your goal is to have a healthy and vibrant lawn. You'll find instructions for doing just that in the pages that follow.

A pole chainsaw, like the one shown here, is ideal for pruning back smaller tree branches that clutter the canopy and create denser shade.

How to Prune a Shade Tree

Start by undercutting from beneath the limb with your bow saw or chain saw.

Finish the cut from above. This keeps the bark from tearing when the limb breaks loose.

Trim the stub from the limb so it's flush with the branch collar, but do not cut the collar, which is responsible for healing the wound.

An electric alligator lopper makes quick work of fallen tree branches. Remove branches quickly; if they're allowed to sit on the lawn too long they can kill the grass underneath and spread diseases.

Removing a Shade Tree

Sometimes, for the health of the lawn, you may choose to remove a tree that has simply grown too large and blocks too much light. But take your time and follow all safety precautions; felling a tree is not a small job. If you don't feel sure of your abilities, hire a professional arborist or tree trimming company to remove the tree. You should definitely seek the help of a professional if the tree is close to the house, or is diseased.

The first step in removing a shade tree is determining where you want it to fall. For safety's sake, you'll also want to decide on two "retreat" paths that will let you avoid the tree if it falls in the wrong direction.

Ensure that tree falls where you want it to by making a series of cuts in the trunk. The first is called a "notch" and is made by cutting out a triangle-shaped section on the side of the tree facing the path you want it to fall along. A felling cut is then made on the opposite side, forming a wide hinge that guides the tree's fall.

Always follow the manufacturer's safety instructions when operating a chain saw. These are extremely dangerous pieces of power equipment and every year, thousands of people are injured using chainsaws. The most common injury is caused by kickback, a sudden movement in which the saw unexpectedly jumps up and back. Kickback is caused by the nose of the guide bar making contact with the tree. Prevent it by avoiding contact with the nose of the guide bar, and using both hands on the handles while making a cut.

Tools & Materials ▸

Chainsaw
Hard hat
Safety glasses
Ear protection

Gloves
Wedge
Hand maul

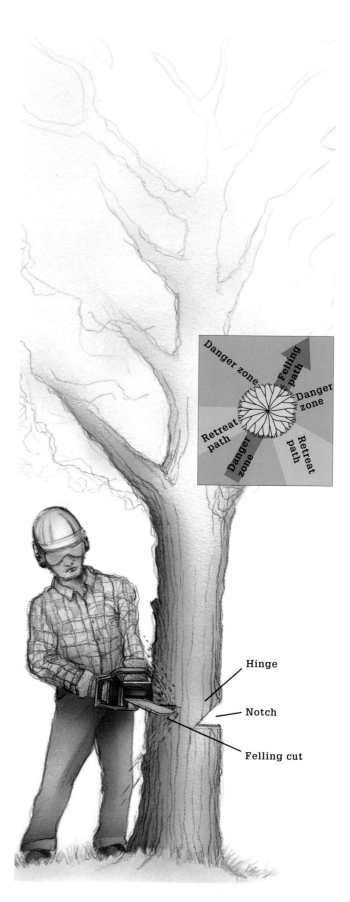

Danger zone

Felling path

Danger zone

Retreat path

Danger zone

Retreat path

Hinge

Notch

Felling cut

How to Fell a Tree

Remove limbs below head level. Start at the bottom of the branch, making a shallow up-cut. Then cut down from the top until the branch falls. *Note: Hire a tree service to cut down and remove trees with a trunk diameter of more than 6".*

Use a chain saw to make a notch cut one-third of the way through the tree, approximately at waist level. Do not cut to the center of the trunk. Make a straight felling cut about 2" above the base of the notch cut, on the opposite side of the trunk. Leave a 3"-thick "hinge" at the center.

Drive a wedge into the felling cut. Push the tree toward the felling path to start its fall, and move into a retreat path to avoid possible injury.

Standing on the opposite side of the trunk from the branch, remove each branch by cutting from the top of the saw, until the branch separates from the tree. Adopt a balanced stance, grasp the handles firmly with both hands, and be cautious with the saw.

To cut the trunk into sections, cut down two-thirds of the way and roll the trunk over. Finish the cut from the top, cutting down until the section breaks away. Do not cut on compressed side of trunk or limb.

Correcting Lawn Drainage Problems

As crucial as water is to the life of a lawn, too much of it can be as bad as too little. A properly draining lawn moves water off the surface rapidly, but slowly enough for grass roots to absorb it. Drainage problems are easy to detect in the form of pooling water, or soil that is moist hours after a rain or watering (or, on the flip side, soil that is bone-dry no matter what you do).

Excess moisture sets the stage for many different diseases and moisture-loving insects, and it stresses the grass. If you see standing pools of water or notice a section of lawn that is squishy underfoot long after you've watered, it's time to pinpoint the cause, which will dictate the solution.

Poor drainage is often a result of soil compaction, in which case regular aeration is the answer. Overwatering by automatic sprinklers can also be a source of excess moisture. That's why the "set-it-and-forget-it" philosophy of automatic sprinkler systems doesn't lend itself to sound lawn-care practice. It pays to regularly check how much water your automatic system is actually spreading on the lawn, using a rain gauge or cans.

The rain gutters and downspouts on your house can also be adding to moisture problems in the lawn. Improperly directed downspouts can create soil erosion that sets up a situation of standing water, or saturation in a given area of the lawn.

Standing water in your lawn is an open invitation to problems from nuisance insects such as mosquitoes, to a full range of damaging lawn diseases.

Grading for Multi-Use Lawns ▸

Lawns are used for a lot of different activities, and grading the soil bed is your opportunity to accommodate special uses. For instance, if you want to add a bocce ball court, volleyball court, putting green, or just a nice, even sitting area, you'll want to grade that particular area so that it is relatively level. Outline the perimeter of the area with evenly placed stakes—a square is the easiest, but you can also outline an oval or circle for a putting green. Extend a string fitted with a line level between a pair of stakes and adjust the string until it's level. Measure down from regular, marked areas of the string to the ground, at 2 ft. intervals. Add and remove topsoil as necessary, redistributing it with a landscaping rake until the surface under the string is level. Repeat the process until the entire area is leveled. If the slope leading to the area is severe and you suspect that water may pool in the level surface, you will need to include a drainage solution— such as a French drain—under the area.

In other cases, the problem may be more endemic; the lawn itself may not be situated for efficient drainage. Properly grading the yard is the first step in ensuring water moves as it should through the lawn. This is best done before you create your new lawn. But even if improper grading is causing drainage problems in an existing lawn, you can use localized solutions such as a French drain, dry bed, or a lawn swale to improve the drainage.

Each of these follows the same basic principle of creating a drainage "field" in the area where moisture is accumulating, to carry away excess water even during heavy rainfall. These solutions can be used regardless of the underlying cause, whether it be a poorly graded yard or clay soil. Drainage can be routed to another area of the garden or yard, off the property into a culvert or gutter, or into a dry well—a simple underground structure that can be highly efficient at draining away excess water.

Whatever the solution, take action as soon as you notice a moisture problem. Excess water in the lawn is one of the more debilitating conditions that can quickly lead to a host of serious problems.

Installing a French Drain

A French drain is a very simple, but very effective solution for poorly draining lawn areas. It involves digging a trench for gravel-covered length of pipe that filters runoff from the lawn, leading it to a low-lying area such as a gutter or wooded section of the property. Never direct a French drain or any other drainage improvement to a neighbor's property.

The most important part of the French drain is the slope. Maintaining a reasonable slope ensures that the runoff will follow the drain. The drain tube itself is covered with permeable landscape fabric. The idea is to allow for water to flow through, while blocking fine soil that could clog up the holes in the drainpipe. Do not use rubber or standard plastic sheeting or pond liners. These will not allow for the free flow of water. You should use clear gravel to surround the pipe for the same reason. Don't use gravel with fines that could clog or block the holes in the drainpipe.

Your tile should underlie the lowest part of the problem area and slope slightly toward an above-grade exit point. Use a 2 × 4 with a level on top to ensure the trench floor carries a gentle downward slope. The trench needs to be at least 1 inch deep where gravel covers it in the problem area. The tile will exit into the gently sloped swale that will carry the water away.

Tools & Materials ▸

Electric edger	Level
Plastic tarp	Turf cutter or garden spade
Gloves	Straight 8' 2 × 4
Tall stakes	4" Perforated drain pipe
Mason's string	¾" (or larger) washed gravel
String level	Permeable landscape fabric
Tape measure	Safety glasses

How to Install a French Drain

Use stakes, mason's string, and a string level to determine a drain path with an above-grade exit point below the level. Use a power edger or spade to cut the turf at the outside edges of the drain trench—usually 8" to 14" wide.

Use a handheld turf cutter or spade to dig up the sod along the trench line. Store the cut sod in a cool, shaded place and moisten regularly while you dig the trench.

Dig out a squared trench over the length of the drain. Place the dirt on a tarp next to the trench site. Use a 2 × 4 with a level on top to ensure the trench slopes slightly to outlet.

Line the bottom of the trench from start to end with permeable landscape fabric wide enough to run 1 ft. up each side. Add about 1" of washed gravel to the bottom of the trench.

Lay perforated pipe (called drain tile) all the way along the trench. Gravel is not needed toward the exit of the tile where the trench becomes shallow.

Add 3" to 4" of gravel on top of the pipe and then fold the edges of the landscape fabric over the top of the gravel and pipe, essentially making an outer sheath of fabric.

Fill the trench with soil, and tamp down, leaving about 1" for the sod. Scratch the top of the soil lightly with a garden rake.

Replace the sod you removed. Roll the sod to ensure firm contact with the soil and water well along the length of the trench. Cover the outlet of the tile with a PVC grate and/or large rocks.

Creating a Drainage Swale

A swale is a very basic drainage solution for an existing lawn. It's essentially a drainage ditch in a natural V of the yard, with a slope that uses gravity to naturally lead water from an area of saturation. The advantages of a swale over more involved solutions such as drainage tiles or French drains is that a swale requires far less excavation, is easier to install, and creates just as nice an appearance as any other drainage option.

As an alternative to a swale—if your yard experiences a significant amount of runoff for may months out of the year—you can create a dry creek. This is essentially a swale without the covering of topsoil and sod. Dry creeks should be half as deep as they are wide and they are often filled with decorative stones, such as polished river rock, and designed as interesting and attractive yard features.

Regardless of the drainage option you choose, you need to contact your local utilities and cable company to ensure that excavation for the planned drainage will not dig up cables or hit pipes.

Tools & Materials ▸

Hammer
Shovel
Wheelbarrow
Spade
Drum roller
Garden fork

Sod cutter (optional)
Gloves
Stakes
Level
Landscape fabric

Filtering Water ▸

A swale can double as a water filter if you install plants with well-established root systems along the entrance area to "clean" water as it runs off into the trench. Grasses planted in the swale dip will clean run-off water (so long as you avoid using chemical lawn care products on this land) before it reaches storm sewers.

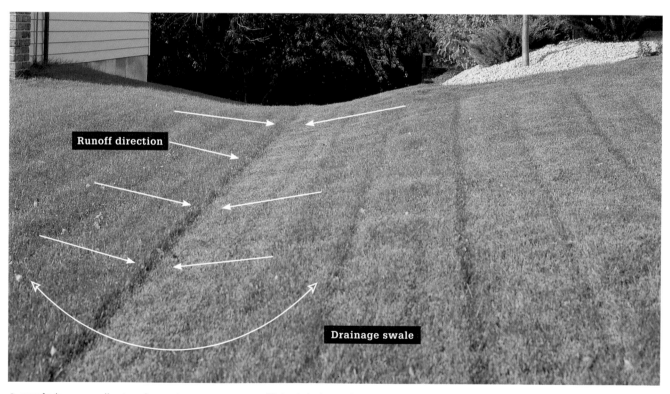

Runoff direction

Drainage swale

A swale is an excellent and easy to way to create efficient drainage for excess runoff water. If your region receives frequent heavy rainfall or if you have clay soil, you may need the more involved solution of a French drain (see page 202).

Swale Options

For severe drainage problems, dig a 1-ft. deep swale angled slightly downward to the outlet point. Line the swale with landscape fabric. Spread a 2"-layer of coarse gravel in the bottom of the swale. Then lay perforated drainpipe over the gravel. Cover the pipe with a 5"-layer of gravel and wrap the landscape fabric over the top of it. Cover the swale with soil and fresh sod. Set a splash block at the outlet to distribute the runoff and prevent erosion.

Gravel comes in two forms: coarse and smooth. When buying gravel for shaping projects, such as drainage swales, select coarse gravel. Coarse gravel clings to the sides of the trench, creating an even drainage layer. Smooth gravel is typically used as a decorative ground cover. When used for shaping projects, it tends to slide toward the middle of the trench.

How to Create a Drainage Swale

Use stakes to mark a swale route that directs water away from the problem area toward a run-off zone. Place stakes slightly uphill from the drainage area.

Remove soil from the marked zone using a shovel. If you must remove grass before digging, consider cutting grass pieces carefully and setting them aside so you can use the turf as sod squares to finish the trench. You can rent or buy a sod cutter to improve your chances of getting reusable cuttings. Otherwise, pile dirt on one side of the trench for a berm.

Shape the trench so it slopes gradually downward toward the outlet, and smooth the sides.

Level the trench by laying a 2 × 4 board with a carpenter's level on the foundation. Distribute soil so the base is level, moving the board to different areas of the trench to check for levelness. Crack the bottom of the swale with a spading fork to aid in percolation (optional).

Lay sod in the trench to complete the swale. Compress the sod and water the area thoroughly to check drainage.

Option: Compact Skidloader

Use the digging attachment on the compact skidloader to move earth. This could mean shearing off the top of a small hill that creates a drainage issue, or excavating to create a natural drainage pattern. Unless you have experience operating utility vehicles, hire a contractor to do this job.

Use a grading attachment on the skidloader to level and move earth. Swales should have very shallow sides and low slopes.

Adding a Mowing Strip

Mowing strips are often considered aesthetic improvements, but they are actually excellent ways to prevent ugly and unhealthy edge compaction in a lawn. They also provide many other benefits for both the lawn and beds and garden plots they butt up against. Not only do these strips provide a stable surface for the wheels of lawnmowers, they also block aggressive weeds and plants such as ivies from invading the lawn, and likewise they prevent strong and healthy turfgrasses from growing into tidy garden beds. Lastly, they form a barrier that prevents runoff—that may contain fertilizer, herbicides, or pesticides—from moving between garden bed and lawn.

So the question is not whether to add a mowing strip but rather, why would you not?

The trick to installing a mowing strip that looks sharp and serves the purpose of a stable platform for your mower's wheels is twofold. First, you should use a solid, strong edging material. Bricks are a great choice, while mulch is less so. Second, you need to make sure the strip itself is reasonably level and firm.

Those aren't hard objectives to achieve if you work steadily and check the strip as you move along. If you lay a brick mowing strip like the one discussed in the steps shown here, it's easy to adjust any mistakes by simply pulling out the offending brick or bricks, adjusting the surface below, and then replacing the bricks. In the same vein, you can fix any unevenness that occurs in settling over time by simply resetting the bricks in their place.

Tools & Materials ▸

Tape measure	Sand
Square-edged shovel	Landscape fabric
Trowel	Bricks
Mallet	2 × 4 scrap

A solid mowing strip is as much protection for flower beds as it is for the lawn. This edge is made from brick pavers set on edge, but many other materials can also be used, including poured concrete, natural stone, or wood timbers.

How to Install a Mowing Strip

Define the edge with a garden hose or spray paint. Even if you're adding a mowing strip in front of an already defined bed as shown here, you'll want to clearly define the edge to make a crisp border.

Cut the edge with a garden spade. Follow the line of the hose and use the spade to dig out a squared up trench about 5" deep, and as wide as the bricks are long.

Line the bottom of the trench with a U-shaped piece of landscape fabric. Fill the bottom of the trench with sand and tamp the sand down evenly, leaving enough space for the bricks to sit level with soil surface.

Set the bricks in place, butting them as tightly together as possible. Check for level side to side and front to back, and adjust as necessary. Spread sand over the bricks and brush it into any gaps between bricks.

Artificial Lawns

Certain areas of your yard might never have been meant to be covered in lush grass. Perhaps there is a great umbrella of shade over a corner of your lawn, cast by old growth oak trees that you wouldn't consider cutting down. Or maybe you've cultivated a stately stand of beautiful, flowering, acid-loving shrubs that require soil conditions that are much too acidic for turfgrass. In some cases, the soil may simply be too barren of vital nutrients, or too rocky, or too sandy to sustain grass plants. And lastly (and perhaps most commonly), local watering restrictions in arid climates may make it impossible to cultivate a living lawn. These are just a few of the landscaping dilemmas to which an artificial lawn may be the answer.

Artificial turf has come a long way since it first came into use in sports stadiums and athletic fields. Although it will never become a completely believable replication of actual grass, today's equivalents to Astroturf are much more realistic than early types. The use of rubberized infill is a particularly good advance that softens the surface underfoot and makes spending time on artificial turf a much more pleasant experience. The introduction of variations in the color and height of individual blades also helps fake turf look much less like the famous backyard of that popular '60s sitcom. Plus, newer products breathe and drain much better, making them more practical for dog owners (they don't discolor or trap odors like outdoor carpet does).

Installing artificial turf is not much more difficult than laying carpet. In fact, in some ways it's easier—it doesn't normally require stretching. An installation about the size of the one shown in the following pages (200 square feet) should take no more than a weekend to do. Turf comes in wide rolls—the EasyTurf product seen here (See Resources, page 218) is sold in 20-ft.-wide rolls—so smaller yard areas can be installed without any seaming. The key is to build a firm, level base for the turf, which will create a natural but stable feel underfoot and will ensure proper drainage. Professionally laid turf bases do this one of two ways—a thick layer of gravel with a sand bed on top; or, a thick layer of sand-and-aggregate mix. Follow the recommendations of your turf's manufacturer or supplier.

Tools & Materials ▸

Measuring tape	as needed
Shovel	Drop spreader
Vibrating plate	Push broom
compactor	Marking spray paint
Landscape rake	Crushed gravel
Tamper	and/or sand
Utility knife	Safety glasses
Seaming materials	Gloves

Synthetic turf has become a much more convincing imitation of natural turf in recent years, making it a viable option for yards (or parts of yards) that are unfriendly to turf grass and in areas where watering restrictions discourage the growing of real grass.

Tiny shady backyards are perfect candidates for artificial turf. Especially for homeowners looking for a good-looking, maintenance-free lawn alternative.

How to Install an Artificial Lawn

Measure the affected area you'd like to cover with artificial turf. Try to find logical starting and stopping points, such as fences and sidewalks. Butting artificial turf up to natural grass seldom gives satisfying results. If it is necessary, however, create a transition feature like a walkway or even landscape edging. Relay the desired dimensions for your artificial lawn to the sales associate at the turf supplier and they'll help you calculate how much material you'll need to order.

Mark off the borders of the area to be covered with landscape spray paint if they do not fall at physical structures. *Tip: If you have a large, flat area outside the project area, roll out the artificial turf so it can lay flat for a few hours prior to installation.*

If your yard has an in-ground sprinkler system, be sure to deactivate and cap off any sprinkler heads in the installation area. Or better yet, disconnect the supply pipes servicing those heads at the manifold.

Excavate to remove existing grass, weeds, and soil to a depth of 3" to 4" (or deeper if your turf manufacturer specifies it).

Level off the soil, using a grading rake. The soil surface should be flat, but if the ground has a natural slope your new turf will normally look best if you allow it to follow the original slope line. *Option: Treat the ground with a liquid herbicide or cover it with landscaping fabric to prevent weed growth.*

Use a plate compactor to tamp the soil base and all other subbase layers after each is laid. Spread the sub-base aggregate across the installation area. Smooth it out with a landscaping rake until it is level, spray with water, and then compact the surface with the compactor, leaving enough room at the top for the thickness of the turf.

Roll out the turf in the installation area. If you need to cut around an obstacle, such as the tree above, roll the turf up to the obstacle, making sure it is in the proper starting position. Then, cut a slit from the opposite edge of the turf so it aligns with the obstacle. Continue rolling. If your plan is for multiple pieces of turf, roll them all out before you do any seaming.

(continued)

Option: Seam the pieces of turf where they meet if you are doing a multi-piece installation or if you had to slice the turf to get around an obstacle. Professional installers typically use special products for seaming artificial turf, but you can do it yourself with supplies available at any building center. First, make sure the pieces of turf are oriented so the naps are facing the same direction and the tuft patterns are aligned. Fold back the turf on both sides of the seam. Cut a strip of building wrap that's about 12" wide and slip it underneath the seam so each half overlays it about 6". Apply a bed of exterior-rated construction adhesive to the building wrap on one half and then set one piece of turf into the adhesive. Move to the other side, apply adhesive, and fold the second half of the turf down into the adhesive (left photo). Press along both sides of the seam to set the parts. For added strength, drive U-shaped landscape fabric staples every 12" along the seam (right photo).

After all seams are complete and you have verified that all turf pieces are exactly where you want them, trim around the borders as necessary. Cut the turf using a utility knife with a new blade or sharp scissors. Here, a concrete paver border has been installed at the edges of the artificial lawn area. Cut the turf just long enough so that the edge can tuck under slightly.

Spread the turf infill recommended by the manufacturer, if any. Sand, small particles of rubber, or a mix of the two are the most common infill materials (also called ballast). For large installations, use a drop spreader to cast the infill.

Use a stiff push broom to spread the infill and help work it into the "root" area of the artificial grass. Monitor the infill as you use your lawn. It occasionally becomes necessary to replenish the material.

Artificial Turf Buying Guide ▸

When shopping for a lawn alternative, keep in mind that not all artificial turf is created equal. Look for a turf that will stand up to your local climate and that doesn't blow your budget. The easiest way to compare different products head to head is to use the square foot cost of the material. Factor in installation costs if you're not doing it yourself, and be sure to add in the extras such as ballast, if you are purchasing that separately.

But you should also be aware of quality differences. If the location you're covering is in direct sun—or if you live in a particularly sunny location—you want to check out how UV-protective different products are. You should also feel the product (most companies offer samples) to see if it's comfortable for bare feet. If you have a pet, you should inquire as to how cleanable and dirt and wear-resistant the turf is. You can get a good sense of these factors based on how long the warranty is for the turf you're considering.

Keep in mind that a comparison between artificial grass and the real thing is hard to make. Although some turf may be a bit pricier to start with, you won't be spending money on fertilizer, weed killer, or other amendments or treatments. You also won't spend any time weeding or mowing.

Use a lawn edger to make clean border and perimeter cuts when removing turf.

Use power loppers to trim windfall into manageable sticks for easy disposal.

Use a blower/vac set on low to suck debris from a mulched bed. The low setting is strong enough to draw leaves up but will leave mulch and other fill material in place.

Use a string trimmer to edge grass along a sidewalk or driveway.

Use a high-powered leaf blower to corral leaves and lawn debris (lower powered blower vacs are intended more for clean-up chores on hard surfaces).

Use electric or cordless hedge trimmers to make fast, even work of hedge and shrub maintenance.

Flip down the bumper attachment on your string trimmer to keep it from getting too close to trees and causing damage to the bark.

Use a power pole pruner to cut through small tree and shrub branches that are out of reach.

Resources

American Lawn Mower Co.
Producers of a full line of reel mowers, in business since 1895.
800-633-1501
www.reelin.com

Black & Decker
Manufactures large selection of corded and cordless electric mowers, trimmers, clippers, cultivators, and other power yard equipment.
www.blackanddecker.com

Cooperative State Research, Education, and Extension Service (CSREES)
(Cooperative Extension System Offices)
Resource center and listing by location of Cooperative Extension Service offices nationwide, as well as consumer information.
www.csrees.usda.gov/Extension

Easy Turf
Producers of artificial turf and related products.
1-866-EASYTURF
www.easyturf.com

Hunter Industries
Manufactures a line of sprinklers and components for in-ground sprinkler systems.
www.hunterindustries.com

Improvements Catalog
Sells inline sprinkler system as seen on page 155.
800-634-9484
www.improvementscatalog.com

Lawn Institute, The
Non-profit corporation that provides education and information on turfgrasses and related topics.
www.thelawninstitute.org

Luster Leaf Products, Inc.
Producers of a range of soil test kits, moisture meters, and rain gauges.
800-327-4635
www.lusterleaf.com

National Turfgrass Federation
National Turfgrass Evaluation Program
In-depth information, research, and evaluation about turfgrass species and related topics.
(301) 504-5125
www.ntep.org
www.turfresearch.org

NaturaLawn of America
Producers and distributors of natural turfgrass products including fertilizers, weed killers, and related products. Also supplies natural lawn-care services.
(800) 989-5444
www.nl-amer.com

Netafim
Supplies irrigation system components for drip and in-ground turf systems.
www.netafimusa.com

Organic Materials Review Institute
Non-profit organization dedicated to ensure the accuracy of organic claims on a full range of consumer products.
541-343-7600
www.omri.org

Rain Bird Sprinkler Systems
Producers of a full range of sprinkler and lawn irrigation systems and components, including electronic rain gauges, digital controllers, and more.
1-800-RAINBIRD
www.rainbird.com

Red Wing Shoes Co.
Work shoes and boots shown throughout book.
800-733-9464
www.redwingshoes.com

Safe Lawns.org
Non-profit organization dedicated to promoting natural lawn-care practices.
www.safelawns.org

Scotts Miracle-Gro Co., The
Producer and distributor of an extensive range of lawn-care products, including Scotts seed and lawn food products, Ortho fertilizers, herbicides and pesticides, and Miracle-Gro fertilizers.
888-270-3714.
www.scotts.com

Turfgrass Producers International
Non-profit trade organization providing consumer education and resources on their website.
www.turfgrasssod.org

Credits

Alamy, (Stocksearch)
p. 149 top, (Nigel Cattlin) pp. 164 left, 165 top, 166 bottom, 167 top, 170 top, 178 right, 180 third from top, 192 top, 192 bottom, 193 bottom left, (Organica) p. 166 left, (JS Photo) p. 175 top

Biocontrol Network,
p. 175 right

John Bria/Lawn Creations,
p. 162 left

William M. Brown Jr., Bugwood.org, p. 191 top

Whitney Cranshaw/Colorado State University, Bugwood.org, p. 183 bottom left

Dirt Works, LLC.
p. 179 top

Dreamstime,
pp. 155 both, 171 bottom, 187 top right and bottom, 200

Arlyn Evans/age fotostock,
p. 181

The Environmental Factor, Inc.,
p. 172 bottom

Florida Division of Plant Industry Archive, Florida Dept of Agriculture and Consumer Services, Bugwood.org,
p. 192 left

Donald Groth, Louisiana State University AgCenter, Bugwood.org,
p. 191 bottom right

Mary Ann Hansen, Virginia Polytechnic Inst. and State University, Bugwood.org,
p. 193 top

iStockphoto,
pp. 64-65; 120, 124, 125 bottom right, 127 both, 134, 138, 139 bottom, 142, 173, 190 left

David Liebman,
pp. 165 left, 183 top left

Bob Mugaas, University of Minnesota Extension Educator, p. 177

Martin Mulder/Getty Images,
p. 160-161

Tim Murphy/University of Georgia, Bugwood.org,
p. 167 bottom left

Ohio State Weed Lab Archive, The Ohio State University, Bugwood.org,
p. 163 top

Photolibrary, (Corbis InsideOutPix) p. 24-25; (Berndt Fischer) p. 187 top left; (Eric Anthony Johnson) p. 189, (JS Sira) p. 190 right, (Francois De Heel) p. 194

Shutterstock,
pp. 13, 23 both, 42, 58, 71 bottom right, 113, 131 top, 140, 162 top and bottom right, 163 middle, 164 top and bottom, 166 top, 167 bottom right, 168 all, 169 all, 170 left and bottom, 171 left and top, 178 left, 180 all except third from top, 182 both, 183 top right, 183 both bottom right, 184 both, 186, 193 bottom right, 195 both

Visuals Unlimited, Inc. (Nigel Cattlin)
pp. 164 bottom right, 191 bottom left

Conversions

Metric Equivalent

Inches (in.)	1/64	1/32	1/25	1/16	1/8	1/4	3/8	2/5	1/2	5/8	3/4	7/8	1	2	3	4	5	6	7	8	9	10	11	12	36	39.4
Feet (ft.)																								1	3	3 1/12
Yards (yd.)																									1	1 1/12
Millimeters (mm)	0.40	0.79	1	1.59	3.18	6.35	9.53	10	12.7	15.9	19.1	22.2	25.4	50.8	76.2	101.6	127	152	178	203	229	254	279	305	914	1,000
Centimeters (cm)							0.95	1	1.27	1.59	1.91	2.22	2.54	5.08	7.62	10.16	12.7	15.2	17.8	20.3	22.9	25.4	27.9	30.5	91.4	100
Meters (m)																								.30	.91	1.00

Converting Measurements

TO CONVERT:	TO:	MULTIPLY BY:		TO CONVERT:	TO:	MULTIPLY BY:
Inches	Millimeters	25.4		Millimeters	Inches	0.039
Inches	Centimeters	2.54		Centimeters	Inches	0.394
Feet	Meters	0.305		Meters	Feet	3.28
Yards	Meters	0.914		Meters	Yards	1.09
Miles	Kilometers	1.609		Kilometers	Miles	0.621
Square inches	Square centimeters	6.45		Square centimeters	Square inches	0.155
Square feet	Square meters	0.093		Square meters	Square feet	10.8
Square yards	Square meters	0.836		Square meters	Square yards	1.2
Cubic inches	Cubic centimeters	16.4		Cubic centimeters	Cubic inches	0.061
Cubic feet	Cubic meters	0.0283		Cubic meters	Cubic feet	35.3
Cubic yards	Cubic meters	0.765		Cubic meters	Cubic yards	1.31
Pints (U.S.)	Liters	0.473 (Imp. 0.568)		Liters	Pints (U.S.)	2.114 (Imp. 1.76)
Quarts (U.S.)	Liters	0.946 (Imp. 1.136)		Liters	Quarts (U.S.)	1.057 (Imp. 0.88)
Gallons (U.S.)	Liters	3.785 (Imp. 4.546)		Liters	Gallons (U.S.)	0.264 (Imp. 0.22)
Ounces	Grams	28.4		Grams	Ounces	0.035
Pounds	Kilograms	0.454		Kilograms	Pounds	2.2
Tons	Metric tons	0.907		Metric tons	Tons	1.1

Converting Temperatures

Convert degrees Fahrenheit (F) to degrees Celsius (C) by following this simple formula: Subtract 32 from the Fahrenheit temperature reading. Then mulitply that number by 5/9. For example, 77°F - 32 = 45. 45 × 5/9 = 25°C.

To convert degrees Celsius to degrees Fahrenheit, multiply the Celsius temperature reading by 9/5, then add 32. For example, 25°C × 9/5 = 45. 45 + 32 = 77°F.

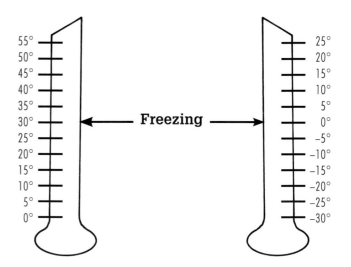

Index

Also From **CREATIVE PUBLISHING international**

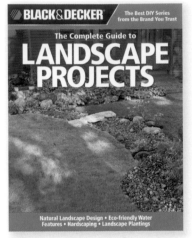

ISBN 978-1-58923-564-9

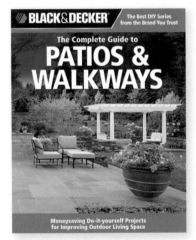

ISBN 978-1-58923-481-9

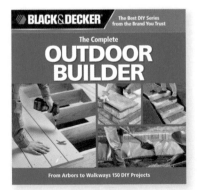

ISBN 978-1-58923-483-3

Creative Publishing
international

400 First Avenue North • Suite 300 • Minneapolis, MN 55401 • www.creativepub.com